Intelligent Design and Fundamentalist
Opposition to Evolution

ALSO BY ANGUS M. GUNN

Evolution and Creationism in the
Public Schools (McFarland, 2004)

Intelligent Design and Fundamentalist Opposition to Evolution

Angus M. Gunn

McFarland & Company, Inc., Publishers
Jefferson, North Carolina, and London

All illustrations are by Paul Giesbrecht

LIBRARY OF CONGRESS CATALOGUING-IN-PUBLICATION DATA

Gunn, Angus M. (Angus Macleod), 1920–
Intelligent design and fundamentalist
opposition to evolution / Angus M. Gunn.
p.   cm.
Includes bibliographical references and index.

ISBN-13: 978-0-7864-2743-7
ISBN-10: 0-7864-2743-4
(softcover : 50# alkaline paper) ∞

1. Evolution (Biology)—Religious aspects—Christianity.
2. Fundamentalism—United States.
3. Intelligent design (Teleology)
I. Title.
BT712.G86   2006
231.7'652—dc22   2006030949

British Library cataloguing data are available

On the cover: Giant panda; detail from the Michelangelo's Sistine Chapel
ceiling fresco *The Creation of Adam;* and portrait of Charles Darwin
(All images from Clipart.com)

Manufactured in the United States of America

*McFarland & Company, Inc., Publishers
Box 611, Jefferson, North Carolina 28640
www.mcfarlandpub.com*

To my fellow evangelicals

Acknowledgments

I thank many friends and authorities for their help in formulating the ideas and opinions expressed in this book. They include members of my family, colleagues from my university, and people from the community where I live. I am particularly grateful for the published expertise from several evangelical scholars in Canada, the United States, Britain, and Australia, and for the ongoing work of the U.S. Center for Science Education (CSE) in the U.S. I discovered over the years that CSE is a loyal watchdog, always active in safeguarding the intellectual integrity of science at all levels of education. Finally, I am glad to see the focus on evolution on the front cover of *Science*, December 2005. The magazine's editorial emphasis, "Evolution in Action," fits perfectly into the content of my last chapter.

Table of Contents

Introduction

I see no conflict between what the Bible tells me about God and what science tells me about nature.
—Francis Collins, Director, National Human
Genome Research Institute, 2005

Maybe it is the rapid pace of change today. Perhaps it is just fear of the future. At any rate fundamentalism, the habit of reverting to or just defending the past, is as alive and well today as it was 40 or even 100 years ago. The past that is defended almost always relates to the infallible and inerrant Bible. Jerry Falwell, one of today's best known fundamentalist leaders and the one who launched the moral majority movement in the 1980s, defined in *The Fundamentalist Phenomenon*, published in 1981, their beliefs and plans. These beliefs and plans, together with their implications for political action, will be analyzed in Chapter 2.

At the opposite extreme there is John Shelby Spong, in whose 1992 book, *Rescuing the Bible from Fundamentalism*, most of the Bible is discounted as ancient mythology with little relevance to our times. It is unfortunate that the title of his book was not reversed because it appears it is the fundamentalists that are in need of rescuing, not the Bible. This book from antiquity has actually stood the test of time and coped well with its critics.

Both of these authors, even if they are not aware of it, are dealing with interpretations of the Bible, not the book per se. Both seem to fail to recognize that their views are time sensitive and should be acknowledged as such. For example, Spong's observation that "a flood covering the known earth to a depth of 25 feet is not a fact of history" would now have to be modified in the light of the recent work of Robert Ballard and others in the Black Sea and Mesopotamia as explained in Chapter 6.

Throughout this book the focus will be on the importance of modern science and the tragedy of fundamentalist rejection of it for such a long time. Humankind tends to pick and choose in science, forgetting that scientific work is one seamless thread through time. Some of the greatest discoveries were made by scientists while working on research that was unrelated to the discoveries. There are high values associated with science for every individual as well as for society as a whole. This is a scientific age that impacts all areas of thought and human dependence on the research and technological development associated with science affects practically every aspect of life. It is read about or its impact is seen on television screens daily at all scales of activity: the exploration of the planet Mars by robots and the various advances in nanotechnology that enable surgeons to deal with all parts of the body with minimal interference, are two examples at polar extremes of contemporary dependence on science.

Sometimes it takes a sudden awareness of danger and with it a demand for scientific help to make society recognize its importance. Within the last decade astronomers observed that a large asteroid was on a possible collision course with earth, an impact that, were it to happen, would destroy more lives than a nuclear war. There are thousands of these asteroids in space and one of them, sometime, will certainly collide with the earth unless human intervention prevents it. Ever since the discovery of the one dangerous asteroid, scientific research has been focused on how to cope with such a future eventuality.

It was thought at first that it might be possible to drive an approaching asteroid off course by sending up a rocket with a nuclear warhead. For various reasons that was discounted as either ineffective or too destructive because of fallout. Conclusions finally settled on the desirability of being able to land an object on an approaching asteroid to change its orbit before it reached earth. See the drawing on page 3: one of the first attempts to test the ability to do this was that which targeted Eros, a 31 mile long asteroid circling the sun almost 300 million miles from earth. Both the target and the rocket sent to intercept it were traveling through space in different directions at enormous speeds. The attempt was successful and others followed in

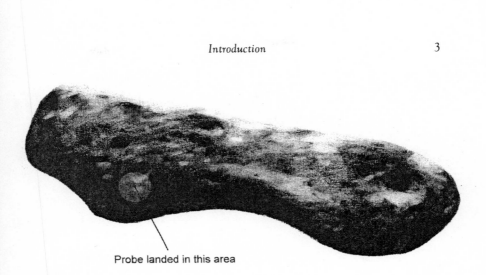

Probe landed in this area

Eros is an asteroid hundreds of millions of miles from earth. The Shoemaker rocket, sent from earth in 2000, successfully made contact with this asteroid in 2001.

later years. Having the ability to land on an object coming toward the earth from space makes it possible to place a reverse thrust engine on that object, one that would slowly, over time, change its orbital course.

The theory of evolution is an indispensable part of modern science. It guides biological research and it illuminates thinking about all aspects of the human body. It gives direction to scientists as they plan animal tests of medicines before approving them for humans. Sometimes there are common genes between animals and humans that relate to a particular medical problem so a cure that works in a lab animal becomes a cure for humans in a very short period of time. The list of medical breakthroughs in Appendix B at the end of this book is one illustration of the many ways in which this Darwinian explanation of life's varieties leads to the medical discoveries on which society depends today. Additionally, as can be seen from this list, the numbers of breakthroughs keep increasing. More and more are occurring within any given span of time. There are more in the second quarter of the 100-year period than in the first and still more in the third than in the second and so on. This is because all discoveries depend on or are helped to some degree by the work of previous researchers.

In spite of all this, for more than 100 years, creationists (now better known as proponents of intelligent design, the fundamentalists of North America) have attacked the theory of evolution as an idea that is harmful. They think it cannot be proven. This is a mean-ingless assertion because science is not in the business of proving any-thing. Instead it concentrates on new things to see what can be disproved rather than proved. The reason that the theory of evolu-tion is so universally accepted today is precisely because it has stood the test of time as scientist after scientist tried to disprove it. Unfor-tunately, ignorance about the nature of the kind of science and sci-entific research that is going on today is widespread and this fact provides opportunities for anti-evolutionists to make all kinds of erro-neous statements such as the following: evolution is in conflict with Biblical interpretations; it defines humans as descendants of apes; it is an attack on traditional morality. The usual response of fundamen-talists to accusations that they are opposed to science is that they are rigorously devoted to experimental or observational science. This is quite true. They do accept the older Baconian or common sense eighteenth-century science which deals with things that can be seen, but they cannot cope with the scientific paradigms of today.

Attacking Evolution All Across America

The map accompanying Chapter 2 is a good indicator of the scale of the anti-evolution activity that is taking place across the United States. One influential intelligent design (ID) leader recently told his followers that unforeseen consequences would follow anyone who made changes to the traditional interpretations of the book of Genesis. In this leader's mind such a change would lead to a break-down in morality. Morality is very high on fundamentalists' agenda so it seems to be difficult for them to understand that morality has nothing to do with scientific studies. Science is and always has been free from issues of ethics or morality. Individual scientists may and do have views on what is right and wrong but these opinions are per-sonal, unrelated to their scientific findings. Some people oppose evo-lution from a different basis than Biblical interpretations. They have a point of view that is similar to that of the eighteenth-century the-ologian William Paley who said that the great complexities we observe in the natural world are proof of an intelligent creator. Paley's thesis ran like this: if a person finds a watch beside a road and examines it, it will soon be evident that its several parts are framed and put together for a purpose. There must have existed at some time and in some place a person who formed it for the purpose it now serves. He then went on to point out that living organisms are more complicated than watches so an intelligent designer must have created them just as only an intelligent watchmaker could have made a watch.

Intelligent design advocates add to Paley's work some of the contemporary findings from molecular biology. (More of Paley's work will be examined in Chapter 5.) Because they do not refer to the Bible at all in their campaign against evolution, they have been able to persuade political leaders to support them. They insist that their opposition has nothing to do with religion, but if that were the case, they would have suggested ID as content for history classes (where ID belongs) rather than science classes. Many of the explanations for past events involve debates about the Bible, or God, or particular interpretations of the Bible. Proofs about a creator have nothing to do with science because they have no supporting experimental evidence and no predictability.

In the summer of 2005, United States President George W. Bush, who wanted to be remembered as the education president, proposed that intelligent design should be taught alongside the theory of evolution to explain the origins of the many life forms existing today. Within days of President Bush's statement, the Senate majority leader, Bill Frist, aligned himself with the president and made the same recommendation. Frist then added that, in a pluralistic society, his and the president's proposal constituted the fairest way to train people for the future.

Any insights into the ways that living things change from one stage to another would be welcomed by biological scientists, but those promoting intelligent design deal only with life's origins and science does not deal with these. The unanswered questions that biological scientists do try to answer all relate to the rate of change among living organisms, to the directions that these changes take from species to species, and to the mechanisms at work effecting change. Chapter 1 will deal with the theory of evolution, covering what is known about it and what is not known. The vast majority of scientists in all countries see no conflict between the theory of evolution and belief in a creator. Furthermore, to return to the position taken by top leaders in the United States, it is entirely inappropriate for political leaders to interfere with the curricula of schools and, at the same time, to contradict the body of scientists who understand the subject. They feel they can do this because there is widespread opposition to evolution across the nation. The National Academy of Science which advises the president on all matters scientific as well as the National Science Teachers Association both support the theory of evolution as the only authentic paradigm for examining different life forms in biological education classes in schools.

Pennsylvania's state curricula in biology are among the very best available anywhere. Nevertheless, even in such a setting, local school boards and individual schools reject these guidelines and impose their own views on schools. Pennsylvania's Dover School Board was one of these in 2005. To make sure that no accurate teaching of evolution would take place, the Board instructed its superintendent to tell biology classes that Darwin's theory is not a fact and that ID is an explanation of the origin of life that differs from Darwin's view. The superintendent was then instructed to tell classes that a copy of a book called *Of Pandas and People* was available for each student. The amateurish nature of the whole routine becomes evident as soon as one reads this book. Its first few lines are as follows: "Intelligent design means that various forms of life began abruptly through an intelligent agency with their distinct features already intact." During the summer and fall of 2005 Dover became a center of interest for the United States. Then, fortunately, in October, in municipal elections, the entire school board was ousted and replaced with representatives who were opposed to the introduction of ID.

A similar story to the Dover episode appeared in 2005 regarding the Cobb County (Georgia) School Board. The Board put a sticker as follows on every text dealing with evolution: "Evolution is a theory, not a fact, regarding the origin of living things. This material should be approached with an open mind, studied carefully, and critically examined." *The New York Times* responded to this in an article titled "The Crafty Attacks on Evolution" with this piece of valuable wisdom: "The only problem with the second sentence is that it singles out evolution as the only subject so shaky it needs critical judgment. Every subject in the curriculum should be studied carefully and critically. Indeed, the interpretations taught in history, economics, sociology, political science, literature and other fields of study are far less grounded in fact and professional consensus than is evolutionary biology."

Farther west in 2005 in the state of Kansas there is a rerun of an old activity. In this case it concerns the duly-elected State Board of Education, not just an errant school district. This Board wants to redefine the state's definition of science, possibly adding supernatural content. In 1999 the Kansas State Board of Education removed the word evolution from the curricula of all of its schools. A year later it reinstated the word but not before the issue of creationism versus evolution had become an issue in the presidential campaign. Both Vice President Gore and George W. Bush defended the Kansas decision when asked. Then, when they discovered that it was in violation of Supreme Court decisions, both men changed their minds and said that subjects like creationism should be taught in some other curricular area. Sadly, political expediency so often is the only value that prevails at the top. Polls keep telling those who run for public office that most Americans want their schools to teach creationism, intelligent design, and evolution together in the same class. Almost as many Americans believe that God created the world and its inhabitants in six days of 24 hours each!

Albert Mohler, president of Southern Baptist Theological Seminary, is a strong supporter of the proponents of ID. The Southern Baptist churches probably form the largest single group of evangelical churches in the country. In a 2005 statement, Mohler points out that God is always involved in every aspect of his creation. Mohler is convinced that creation occurred in six days, in the present meaning of these words, and he rejects any suggestion that humans evolved from nonhuman species. Both Mohler and Michael Behe, who is a leader in the ID movement, define the mechanism of evolution as Darwin defined it, a mechanism that is no longer part of the theory of evolution. This is an old technique that is used when anti-evolutionists want to win an argument; they pick a straw man that can easily be defeated. Richard Dawkins, Britain's foremost authority on the theory of evolution, was asked what he thought about the ID movement. He rejected it as completely unscientific and added, in relation to its fundamental claim that there must be a designer: "Who designed the designer?"

This Book Chapter by Chapter

The first two chapters deal with the central themes of the book, the nature of modern science as exemplified in the theory of evolution and the characteristics of contemporary fundamentalists who, among other things, oppose evolution, not with regard to its central feature but rather concerning the mechanism that Darwin recommended. Those involved forget that Darwin's mechanism is no longer the only process at work. Chapter 1 therefore emphasizes the great difference between Darwin's theory of evolution and the ongoing debates over mechanisms. It also deals with erroneous applications of Darwin's theory to social conditions. Chapter 2 traces the history of fundamentalism. Throughout that history, morality was a dominating theme, so it is examined in some detail.

The next two chapters deal with two modern developments that threaten fundamentalism: one is the higher criticism of the Bible and the other is evolution. In both of these chapters, Chapter 3 regarding higher criticism of the Bible, and Chapter 4 regarding evolution, we encounter the clearest examples of the root historical meaning of fundamentalism. It stands for no change. In other words let all things remain as they were 200 years ago.

Chapter 4 is the heart of the book. It contains descriptions of *The Fundamentals*, the 12-volume library that was funded by the Stewart brothers and distributed to millions of Christian workers throughout the English–speaking world. Ninety authors were involved in the writing and the plan was to stop the tide of modernism that seemed about to overwhelm all evangelicals. It shows how Fundamentalism is finally and clearly identified for all America and for the rest of the twentieth century. The defining event was the Scopes Trial. It marked evolution as the great enemy of fundamentalists, a mark that is evident in all the present anti-evolution opposition all over the nation. Chapter 3, in addition to the issue of higher criticism, deals with the story of Scottish common sense science, or Baconian science, the science of Newton and of Jefferson which contributed to the uniting of evangelicals and the nation's political leaders at the time of independence.

Chapter 5 picks up the story of fundamentalism, clearly defined after the Scopes Trial, and traces its development for the rest of the century and beyond. This period of time saw the emergence of all kinds of so-called scientific alternatives to evolution: creationism, creation science, flood theology, and now intelligent design. Chapter 6 examines the meanings of Biblical interpretations. The central point here is that almost all disagreements about the Bible are disagreements about particular interpretations rather than Biblical accuracy. To illustrate this point the early chapters of Genesis are shown to be clear statements of transcendental communications and nothing more. Thus the accusations of conflicts between these parts of the Bible and the findings of modern science are irrelevant. Fundamentalists, and there are many of them today, who insist that these chapters are historically accurate, lose all credibility. Chapter 7, the last one, illustrates, via case studies, the ways in which the theory of evolution is beneficial to human welfare.

Understanding Modern Science

Because this book is all about a problem in science, readers need to understand what scientists all over the world mean by the word science and the phrase scientific method. Science is only one form of knowledge and it often uses words that carry meanings that are quite different from their meanings in other settings. Familiarity with both scientific language and scientific methods will help us greatly as we go on, in Chapter 1, to study what the theory of evolution is and what it is not. A good beginning is the definition of science given by the (U.S.) National Science Teachers Association. This organization is anxious to see good science being taught in schools and it keeps up to date with all new developments in other scientific associations. Here is its definition of science: "It is a method of explaining the natural world. It assumes that anything that can be observed or measured is amenable to scientific investigation. Science also assumes that the universe operates according to regularities that can be discovered and understood through scientific investigations. The testing of various explanations of natural phenomena for their consistency with empirical data is an essential part of the methodology of science. The most important scientific explanations are called "theories." In ordinary speech, "theory" is often used to mean "guess" or "hunch," whereas in scientific terminology, a theory is a set of universal statements that explain some aspect of the natural world." Fortunately this word is used so widely in society that most dictionaries now define it in its scientific sense and give illustrations from science of where it fits, such as atomic theory, economic theory, theory of evolution, or theory of equations.

The following definition of science comes from the Australian Science Teachers Association. It is similar in many ways to the United

States one which is given above. The impetus for the Australian teachers issuing it came from a decision by the Australian Minister of Education to add intelligent design to the biology curricula of schools. "The study of science is about what is measurable, testable and evidence-based. Scientific theories are subject to testing and are modified on the basis of facts and experimental evidence. The theory of evolution is the best scientific explanation for explaining the changes in life on Earth. As with any scientific theory, the theory of evolution will continue to be modified as new observations and discoveries are made. Intelligent Design is a belief system that maintains that certain features of the universe and living things are best explained by the intervention of an intelligent cause. As with any religion or system of belief, it may warrant a place in a religious or cultural studies curriculum. It does not have a place in a science curriculum, alongside scientific theories such as evolution. As it is not possible to set up an experiment to test Intelligent Design, it cannot have any status as a scientific theory and hence has not been included in science curriculum in Australia."

It is difficult to understand the lack of knowledge about modern science throughout the United States. Compared with the United States, no nation on earth had as rich and as sustained an exposure to excellence in the teaching of science for most of the twentieth century. American education was dominated by the ideas of John Dewey throughout that time, the man whose expertise in the teaching of science received acclaim in America and throughout the world. His publications were more numerous and more widely translated in other languages than those of any other scholar within the past 400 years. The main features of Dewey's methods are described in *Evolution and Creationism in the Public Schools*, published by McFarland in 2004. When major national scientific projects were launched in the 1960s by the United States National Science Foundation in the wake of the flight of the Russian spacecraft, Sputnik, John Dewey's methods dominated the findings of the various projects that were conducted in physics, earth science, biology, and anthropology. In the years that followed, however, in the 1970s and 1980s, few educational authorities made use of the results of these valuable scientific endeavors. What went wrong? Why was Dewey so successful until 1960 but not today? The answer lies in an opposition to modern science especially to the theory of evolution, by a majority of Americans. The theory of evolution was introduced to the schools in the 1960s to ensure that the U.S. would compete more successfully with the Soviet Union. Because so many Americans opposed it, the nation's leaders also rejected it.

A good illustration of modern scientific methods comes from Darwin's experiences when sailing in the south Pacific, many years before he wrote *Origin of Species*. Like great scientists before him, Darwin was always curious about things he saw in nature that puzzled him. So, when he observed atolls for the first time, he began to ask questions: How did they originate? Why are they all circular in form? Atolls are rings of coral islands surrounding areas of shallow water called lagoons and they are a common sight in the south Pacific. Darwin's first guess was that they were craters of extinct volcanoes that now lie below the surface on which coral polyps had built up ridges over time. In science, the word "hypothesis" is used instead of "guess" because "hypothesis" includes some evidence in support of one's thinking. The sailors on the ship, in response to Darwin's hypothesis, measured the depth of the water on the ocean side of the lagoon and found it went down to great depths. They also discovered coral down as far as 60 feet and, after that, a mixture of coral and sand for the next 120 feet. Beyond that depth, there was no coral and sand mixture. It seemed that Darwin's hypothesis was an accurate estimate of the origin of the atoll. Now read the top of page 4 of this introduction and note that science is always seeking to disprove hypotheses rather than prove them. The reason for this is that scientists want to discover new knowledge that cannot be disproved no matter how many new things are discovered.

Later, on the same voyage, at another atoll, sailors examined the water outside the lagoon and discovered the remains of the corals as far down as 4,000 feet. This immediately destroyed Darwin's first hypothesis because it was well known that corals do not live at that depth. New hypotheses were required. Darwin was unable to offer another hypothesis at that time and soon his work took him in new directions. However, others were very interested in what he had initiated and they followed up on it. About 40 years after Darwin's first effort, an oceanographer who specialized on the effects of the last ice age on the levels of the oceans came up with a new hypothesis; he had discovered that ocean levels dropped by 300 feet at the height of the ice age so he proposed that corals slowly built up ridges on the edges of volcanoes during that time. This was an interesting hypothesis but, like Darwin's original one, it did not fit all the facts. Coral remains had been found 4,000 feet below sea level. Thus the second hypothesis had to be discarded. It took another 80 years, long after the death of Darwin, before the puzzle was solved. That happened in the 1960s when the great tectonic plates on the sea floor were discovered. One of the largest of these is the Pacific Plate. It moves westward across the Pacific Ocean and where there is an opening beneath it, as in Hawaii, huge volumes of lava rise slowly to the surface to form islands. The islands cool slowly as the plate moves on and they sink. Their enormous weight takes them down to great depths. Coral remains built up on them when they were near the surface travels down with them. Not every scientific problem takes more than 100 years to be validated and become a theory, but the processes involved are always the same whether it takes an hour, a year, or centuries for validation.

1

Understanding the
Theory of Evolution

There is grandeur in this view of life, with its several powers, having been originally breathed by the Creator into a few forms or into one.

—Charles Darwin, 1859

There is a temptation for those who oppose evolution to think of this important aspect of biological science as an idea that appeared suddenly in Darwin's mind in the middle of the nineteenth century. The facts of the case are quite different. What Darwin proposed in his famous book *The Origin of Species* was the end product of many years of research by him and by the many others who came before him, as well as by those with whom he consulted and who critically assessed his work. There were endless debates for and against Darwin's thinking before it became a theory (in the scientific sense of that word) as so often happens in scientific advances. Rarely does an important new discovery appear in its finished form at one moment in time. Some aspects of Darwin's conclusions were overtaken by later research and changed. What remained and was confirmed again and again by thousands of researchers is the paradigm we know as "the theory of evolution." The DNA molecule (see next page) was the final confirmation of it in the 1950s. This book will examine some of the ramifications of DNA later in this chapter. First, here are some of the developments that led up to the final publication of 1859.

13

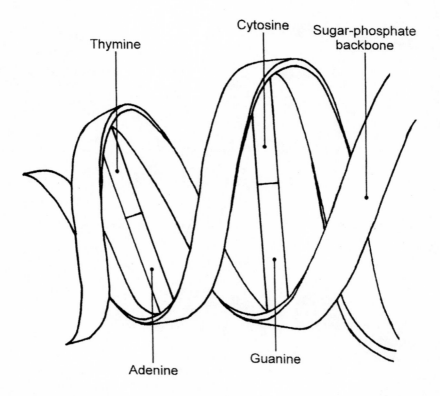

The DNA molecule consists of two interlocking strands of sugar and phosphate with different arrangements of four nucleotide bases (the genes) between them.

Before Darwin

Some ideas about heredity were known in the middle of the eighteenth century. Doctors knew that each parent contributed what they called "particles" to the next generation but there was little understanding of their composition. Sometimes the particles from one parent were dominant and at other times they appeared two or three generations later. The word "Darwinism" or something like it entered the English language long before Charles Darwin was born. Erasmus Darwin, Charles' grandfather, a doctor, wrote a book at the close of the eighteenth century called *The Laws of Organic Life*, in which he hoped to explain the history of diseases. Like most scientific writings of that time, there was a good deal of speculation and very little factual information in this book. The author's references in it to animals constantly changing hinted at some kind of evolutionary theory, but the lack of any supporting data led instead to the coining of the word "darwinizing," meaning random guessing.

Jean Baptiste, or Chevalier de Lamarck, of France (1744–1829), was another pre–Charles Darwin figure who studied and wrote about biology. His views on evolution were first published in 1809, the year of Charles Darwin's birth. Lamarck described certain laws of development that determine changes in successive generations of animals. In his view, a giraffe develops a long neck by constantly having to strain upward to get food from trees. Small changes occur in this way in a giraffe's neck in the course of a lifetime, and Lamarck posited that these changes are passed on to offspring. Lamarck believed that over long periods of time, these changes lead to the emergence of new species. This thesis of Lamarck's—changes occurring in the life of an animal are passed on to the next generation—was very popular. In later years, Charles Darwin was attracted to it and it became a firm conviction for the rest of his life. It affected his view of the mechanisms determining evolution, a view that was controversial in his lifetime and one that is still undetermined. Now that scientists have DNA together with all kinds of additional research findings, it is known that Lamarck and those who accepted his ideas were wrong. Characteristics acquired in one lifetime are not passed on to the next one.

When Lamarck died in 1829, Georges Cuvier, the influential French biologist, said that his work had no value. Cuvier, who became known for his support of catastrophism, was convinced that species were fixed and never changed. He believed that earth's history was a series of catastrophes with new species arising after each one of these cataclysmic events. He came to Paris in 1795 after the disruptions of the revolution had faded so he was able to devote his energies to scientific work. He, like some others of his time, was anxious to establish science as a separate discipline, quite independent of philosophy or theology. That was difficult in his time. Other scientists who had attempted to do this were defined as atheists. Cuvier joined the staff of the Museum of Natural History in Paris and launched into a study of earth's history through examining fossils. He emphasized the importance of empirical evidence in his writings and criticized other naturalists who failed to provide supporting experimental evidence in their writings. This may have been the main reason for his opposition to Hutton, whose work will be examined later, but his devotion to the theory of catastrophism was undoubtedly another. One of his main contributions to science was his classification of animals into four basic types.

Lamarck held some creative views on evolution later in his life. They lacked experimental evidence so they were rejected in his lifetime, but they have links with a few modern developments. Lamarck became convinced that organisms have a built-in tendency to become increasingly complex. He wrote about this, describing it as an inner force operating continuously for the improvement of the species. He contended that it ran right through the history of life on earth and culminated in the emergence of the human species. Charles Kingsley (1819–1875), an author and social reformer in England, held similar views after the lifetime of Lamarck. He, like so many others of his time, saw everything in terms of direct action by God. His view was that God had originally given a built-in capacity to organisms to develop along certain lines. Still later, in the 1990s, with significant experimental evidence to back up his thinking, Conway Morris of Cambridge published his ideas on convergence, a concept that explained intelligent responses by life forms to the challenges they faced in their different environments. Conway Morris is an expert on the Burgess Shale, the place in Eastern British Columbia where discoveries were made of a huge deposit of fossils from the Cambrian Period of 500 million years ago. Conway Morris is presently Professor of Evolutionary Paleobiology at the University of Cambridge.

From Scotland in 1844 came the publication *Vestiges of the Natural History of Creation* by Robert Chambers, a book dealing with the same issue others had tried to answer: how organic forms change from generation to generation. Chambers' answer was more imaginative than factual, depending in large part on what he called the natural way of development of everything in the universe. In his mind everything evolved from a lower state to a higher one, or from a simple form to a more complex one. He used the stages of development of a mammal as it was progressively modified in the womb from an embryo to a live animal to illustrate his idea. He concluded that these changes of organic forms were due to the action of a personal and intelligent God who worked through a system of laws. His work was discounted by the geologist Adam Sedgwick, Darwin's former teacher at Cambridge, and by Thomas Huxley who said that Chambers had a thoroughly ignorant and unscientific mind. Chambers' book was widely distributed and his reference to natural laws of development tended to confuse public understanding of Darwin's work when it appeared and attributed causation to natural selection.

There are also cases of phony scientists who imitated Lamarck. In the Soviet Union, from the 1930s until it was finally abandoned in the 1960s, Trofim Denisovich Lysenko picked up an aspect of Lamarck's thinking and was able to hoodwink the Soviet government into accepting a new agricultural technique called vernalization, using humidity and low temperatures to make wheat grow in Spring. It was not really new. It had been tried before and found to be useless, but the Soviet authorities were desperate to find an answer to a crisis in agriculture, so they accepted his plan. Lysenko promised to triple or even quadruple wheat yields. He used peasant reports rather than experimental evidence to justify his theory and in the 1930s Soviet propaganda was anxious to cover up the horrors of collectivization with stories of peasants being successful with agricultural innovations. The violent collectivization of farms in the Ukraine had destroyed farming and killed millions through famine or deportation to death camps, so the government was anxious to do anything that would restore productivity to the formerly-rich wheat-growing areas of the Ukraine. Carl Sagan once compared American creationists to Lysenko because they allowed political interests to subvert true science.

These names are illustrative of the long-standing interest in the ways that important characteristics and appearances of living things are passed from one generation to another. The ideas of one of them, those of Lamarck, contributed in a negative way. This negative is Lamarck's conviction that characteristics acquired in a lifetime are passed on to succeeding generations, something that was accepted by Darwin. Lamarck's ideas left Darwin somewhat confused about the mechanisms involved in the changes in life forms over time. These processes of change will be examined in greater detail later.

There are two other scientists whose work related directly to the theory of evolution. This does not mean that there is a linear connection between their contributions to science and the things that Darwin discovered. Advances in scientific discovery do not usually work like that as mentioned in the introduction. In the cases of these two scientists whose stories follow, the work of one of them, Gregor

Mendel, was linked to the subsequent discovery of DNA. The other, James Hutton, provided the theory of uniformitarianism, an important perspective which was picked up later by Charles Lyell who, in turn, expanded it to assist Darwin in designing his mechanism of natural selection.

Gregor Johann Mendel (1822–1884) could have been one of Darwin's most valuable precursors had he met him. They were contemporaries but they never got to know each other. The name Gregor was added to his birth name, Johann Mendel, when he was ordained into monastic life. In the monastery, his new home, he spent a big part of the time experimenting with pea plants. He isolated those with distinctive characteristics, interbred them, and checked to see which characteristics of the original reappeared in the next generation. In one experiment he crossbred yellow peas with green ones and found a first generation of all-yellow peas. Subsequently he discovered that the greens reappeared in a later generation. The yellow peas had clearly been dominant and the green ones recessive. Mendel continued his work with thousands of pea plants and came to the conclusion that parental characteristics were always transmitted as intact factors not, as might be expected, as blended colors which is what would happen if someone mixed paints of different colors. In 1866 Mendel presented his findings to the Natural History Society of Bonn. From there it was distributed to a hundred learned societies in different countries. His work was a purely mathematical summary of how different factors are transmitted in their entirety to a succeeding generation. As such it was an important step toward the discovery of genetics.

James Hutton (1726–1797) was a Scottish doctor who traveled widely throughout Britain studying rocks and collecting fossils from different rock formations, searching for information on the geology of the past. He had questions about the prevailing view of earth's history, that it was a recent creation, only thousands of years old, and that the form of its surface was the result of violent eruptions. Near his home in eastern Scotland, Hutton had found layers of sandstone and shale close to the surface, all of them either vertical or folded back on one another. The common view of the time that these layers were formed by one or even several upheavals from the past seemed to him to be a completely inadequate explanation. He was familiar with processes of erosion because he lived on a farm and had seen the effects of rivers on the landscape. He compared the tiny fragments of rocks that they carried from higher ground and deposited at their mouths to the rocks in the layers of sandstone. They were identical rock types but with one important difference: the vertical and twisted layers of rock had been subjected to great pressure to such an extent that they had become solid rock instead of collections of tiny rocks. From observations like these Hutton concluded that the solid layers of sandstone or shale must have emerged from the work of rivers in the past, that they once were deposits at the mouths of rivers just like the ones he saw on his farm, and that somehow they were compacted into their present solid form and uplifted.

It gradually became clear to Hutton that an enormous amount of time must have elapsed for these things to happen. In 1795 he compiled and published his book, *Theory of the Earth*, in which, perhaps for the first time in history, he proposed a very great age for the earth, so great that he could only define it as having no vestige of a beginning and no prospect of an end. He urged people to stop thinking of time by the clock in the church steeple and look instead at the clock in the mountains. Hutton had no way of measuring the actual age of the earth. Techniques based on radiation by which the earth's age is known today were not available in his lifetime. Nevertheless, the science of geology was born as a result of Hutton's efforts and he is today regarded as its founder. Like all scientists of his time, Hutton was a firm believer in the Bible. He saw the cycles of erosion and subsequent uplift of rocks as God's way of renewing the surface of the earth to make it a self-perpetuating home for humanity. The concept of uniformitarianism is derived from Hutton's work. This view is in sharp contrast to Cuvier's theory of catastrophism because it asserts that the processes we see operating today were the norms of yesterday. Cuvier, who was a well-known scientist, rejected Hutton's theory because it was not based on experimental evidence and he was able to delay its acceptance for more than 50 years. Today, with the knowledge of tectonic plates, among other things, Hutton's findings are fully vindicated.

Charles Lyell (1797–1875), the son of a rich landowner, studied at Oxford and then at the age of 21 took an interest in geology and joined the Geological Society. He soon gained the reputation of being an advocate of Hutton's theory of uniformitarianism. His great influence in Darwin's life distinguishes him from all the other scientists who contributed in one way or another to the theory of evolu-

tion. Uniformitarianism allows for part of Cuvier's claim that cata-
strophic events did shape the earth's surface in the past, but only over
short stretches of time in the aggregate. Most of earth's history according to uniformitarianism happened gradually and, as has been said,
in ways similar to the forces seen at work today. Lyell was the first to
make extensive use of Hutton's findings and it became central to Darwin's work as will be demonstrated. There was very little awareness
of the great age of the earth in the first half of the nineteenth century and here again Lyell was the pioneer investigator. His *Principles
of Geology, Volume Two* carried a diagram that listed the geological eras
of Cenozoic, Mesozoic, and Paleozoic and he had given names to parts
of these that are still in use today. Miocene, Pliocene, and Eocene are
names of epochs within the Cenozoic era that were given by Lyell.
His drawing of the Paleozoic Era was marked as extending beyond 400
million years. No one had previously suggested an age for the earth
anywhere close to that figure and when Darwin suggested an age similar to that of Lyell's he had to withdraw it because of opposition
from many scientists.

A great age for the earth gradually became an essential component of the theory of evolution because of the natural selection mechanism that Darwin had chosen. Lyell's adoption of Hutton's work
along with his additional research in geology and biology were published in his first volume of *Principles of Geology* which he completed
at the age of 23. When Darwin, at the age of 22, left for his five-year
exploratory voyage on the *Beagle*, one of the important books he took
with him was Lyell's *Volume One* which his friend John Henslow gave
him as a going away gift. Lyell became a strong formative influence
in Darwin's thinking all through his time on the *Beagle* and for years
afterward. In the course of the journey around South America, Darwin received Lyell's second volume of *Principles of Geology*, while on
the east coast, and the third volume while in Chile on the west side.
These books provided the background for all of Darwin's thinking
about the processes of nature. There was great value to Darwin in
Lyell's second volume because it went beyond geology and applied the
theory of uniformitarianism to biology. It showed how the ages of
rocks could be determined by the fossils they contained. By so doing
he continued to extend still farther back the common view of the age
of the earth. A drawing in his second edition linked different fish and
animals with geological periods. For a long time after *Volume Three* of

his book was published, Lyell remained convinced that the old view of species being fixed was true. He had difficulty explaining the presence of new ones.

Darwin the Theologian and Scientist

Charles Darwin was born on February 12, 1809, in England. Like Churchill or Einstein or so many other great achievers throughout history, he was bored with the limited challenge at school and remembered little from his days there. One of his few memories related to watching birds. His father, a doctor, was very disappointed about his poor performance at school, so he sent him to Edinburgh, at the age of 18 (not an unusual age for that time) to study medicine. Darwin was as disinterested with studies there as he had been at school and spent much of his time with friends examining natural history. After two years he persuaded his father to let him leave medicine and allow him to move to Cambridge and take up preparation for church ministry. One of the things that troubled Darwin while studying medicine was the necessity of observing operations without anesthetic. Chloroform was not yet available. Modern people are inclined to ask, why did his father have to choose a career for his son? Could he not choose for himself? That option was not available. In the first half of nineteenth century England parental control of family members was the norm among middle class families and little choice was available to a young person until he or she was firmly established in a profession. At Cambridge Darwin was again a disappointment to his father. He skipped classes and spent a lot of time collecting beetles. He finally managed to gain a pass degree in theology.

His first degree in theology was the only academic degree he ever earned. As was the custom of the time at the universities of Cambridge and Oxford, he later received a master's degree on payment of a fee, something that today might be called a sort of honorary master's. It's a practice with which most North Americans are not familiar. The Scottish universities have a different system of degrees. There is no bachelor degree and the first degree awarded is a master's. The only reason for mentioning these things is to help with understanding the strong and lasting background he had in theology. It was a background with which he had to contend as he found his scientific work clashing with all he had studied and believed about God. He was never disrespectful of, or insensitive to the convictions of friends who were Christians. Some of them were very close to him and with one of them he shared his proposed theory of evolution years before he presented it publicly. The sharp contrast seen between Darwin's courteous and considerate approach to those with whom he disagreed and the caustic, odious language employed by so many evangelical Christians against him is a sad commentary on the modern social world (both its recent past and its present). In the year he graduated, the same year in which he was appointed as naturalist for the planned exploratory voyage of the *Beagle*, Darwin could be described as a person who accepted the tenets of the Anglican Church in which he grew up. He had no revolutionary ideas about nature that contradicted the commonly held views about God's direct involvement in the natural world.

His real interests lay in the natural world, so the five-year voyage (which will be examined a little later as the key to the flowering of Darwin the scientist) became the first set of experiences that matched the kind of work he had longed to do. It also became the source of the extended conflict that developed between his Christian background and the scientific ideas that were emerging from his observations while on the *Beagle*. This conflict became focused in the years that followed the voyage as his theory of evolution took shape. It became a source of tension between him and his friends. The details of his thinking and some of his interactions and correspondence with others regarding the reality or otherwise of God as an active agent in the natural world have great value today. This is important for several reasons, as society has to cope at the present time with a mindless fundamentalism that makes extravagant claims about the activities of God based on a literal reading of the Bible. For the most part these claims are not derived from personal study and the convictions that emerge from it. Instead they represent long-standing customs and beliefs that constitute a tradition, one that has not changed very much in centuries. There are also concerns that relate to the authoritarian influence of institutional Christianity that inhibit clear thinking about the issue of God or no God in the study of the natural world. Darwin's experience can be a valuable help in these situations.

The only evidence of a serious interest in theological issues during his academic studies at Cambridge relates to William Paley's writings. The book that was required reading, *The Evidences of Christianity*, fascinated him because it appealed to rational thought, in contrast to the volumes of information on church history and practice that he had to study. He later reflected on Paley's writings, including his *Natural Theology*, describing them as giving as much delight as did the study of geometry. The tight logic that Paley expressed in his books was so much welcomed by Darwin that he memorized the entire content of *The Evidences of Christianity* as he prepared for examinations. The mind of a scientist, the attractiveness of data that could be analyzed and assessed rationally, was clearly in evidence at this stage of Darwin's life. The subject would not appear again for some time after his return from the *Beagle*. Many changes had taken place in his thinking during the five-year voyage and this, together with the huge volume of material he had collected, kept him busy for most of the time over the following 10 years. He was happily married with a family during those years and family wealth enabled him to devote his time to the analysis of the biological material he had brought back in the *Beagle*. In the fall of 1850, 14 years after his return from the voyage, intellectual questions about God began to surface again and he decided to step aside from his work to do some reading. All of Francis William Newman's major works were studied.

Francis was the brother of John Henry Newman and both men had created quite a stir in the intellectual life of England by walking away from the Anglican Church, John Henry to join the Catholic Church and later to become Cardinal Newman, and Francis to launch out in new ways, seeking rational alternatives to the dogma with which he had been brought up. Some aspects of the 39 articles of the church bothered him, particularly the notions of future reward and punishment based on one's performance in this life. He could not stay in the church and still raise questions about the church's articles, so he left. He wrote several popular books that outlined his spiritual journey toward a more general theism which culminated in a dedication to personal devotion. The rationality of Newman's writing appealed to Darwin, but in the midst of his reading activity, Darwin had to cope with a domestic crisis. Darwin's 10-year-old daughter Annie, to whom he was strongly attached, had been ill for some time and became so much worse that she had to be sent to a special medical clinic. Darwin spent days at her bedside, deeply troubled about her condition. Within a month of her stay at the clinic, she died. Darwin grieved greatly, quit his reading, and returned to his scientific research. There was little doubt in his mind, given his behavior and words at the time and afterward, that God, if he existed, could and should have kept Annie alive. It is here that the failure of the church becomes clear.

For more than 1,000 years, Christianity was defined in society by the edicts of the major institutional organizations (such as the Anglican in more recent times and the Catholic church for all of that time). Ideas relating to individual freedom of thought and personal responsibility had largely been replaced by the requirement of submission to the rites and belief systems of these institutions. All that was demanded of individuals was acceptance of the church's rules and, if they did, individuals were assured of a safe transfer to the afterlife. This is still the condition in some Christian institutions just as it is among fundamentalists. For the latter it is not so much an institutional thing as a rejection of rationality and acceptance of indefensible dogma. For thoughtful people today, just as it was with Darwin, these approaches to truth are unacceptable. They argue that, if there is a creator and if he created rational beings, then he would expect them to use their minds whenever important matters had to be understood. Fortunately there has been a great deal of progress within the Christian community since Darwin's time. At least some organizations now expect people to think through the implications of the information they receive about God or about creation. Without adequate thought and reflection, a person becomes an easy target for every charlatan that comes along.

Nine years after Annie's death and after his life's work, *The Origin of Species*, had been published and widely distributed, Darwin found himself, unfortunately, defending the one mechanism of evolution that he was convinced was the true one, namely natural selection. Today we know that that was a wrong view but, of course, it did not affect the validity of his thesis. He had a good friend, Asa Gray, a Christian biologist with whom he first shared his thesis many years before it was published and who accepted natural laws as God's way of accomplishing evolution. In correspondence with Gray on the subject of God's involvement or noninvolvement in nature, Darwin wrote that he could not see as plainly as others do evidences in nature of design and beneficence. He had previously reported on examples of cruelty that he had observed in nature. Nevertheless, Darwin insisted, he could not remain content with a view that saw humans as the result of brute force.

There is double tragedy in all of these tensions in Darwin's life over God's role in nature. First there was the presumption in Darwin's mind, as there is in so many others, that the character of God can be defined, if God exists, and to consider God as non-existent if God does not fit the given definition. Second, as stated previously, the church of his time failed Darwin by offering a picture of God that was too anemic for any thinking person to accept. Darwin finally ignored his church's views, put aside discussions about God, and pursued his scientific work.

The great achievers from history were often bored with school. It never seemed to challenge their abilities adequately but, by good fortune, it often happened that their interests and abilities were identified and nourished by incidental contacts with mentors. This was true for some like Churchill and Einstein, and it turned out fortuitously for Darwin at Cambridge. His interest in nature brought him into contact with John Henslow, professor of botany, and they became good friends. About the time that Darwin graduated in church ministry and had just returned home, Henslow received a request from the captain of a ship that was about to sail for South America and the Pacific to conduct a hydrographic survey. The captain needed a naturalist and Henslow immediately recommended Darwin who, as we can guess, was delighted at the prospect. His father, however, was totally opposed to this prospect and only the intervention of Darwin's uncle, Josiah Wedgwood, made it possible for him to go. Wedgwood was able to persuade Darwin' s father that the survey would be a valuable experience for a clergyman. Thus it happened that Darwin left England in 1831 for the momentous five-year voyage that would change his life. It sounded ideal but throughout the entire five years he was always seasick. To his credit, his devotion to naturalistic studies never faltered. He studied everything, from terrain conditions to the smallest insects, and compiled thousands of pages of notes.

Darwin left England convinced that different species were fixed realities, so ordained by their creator, and returned in 1836 with considerable doubt about it. He married his first cousin Emma and settled down in London to sort out the enormous amount of material that had been collected and enjoying, while there, extensive contacts with the nation's leading scientists and scientific organizations. It took 10 years to sort out the information from the *Beagle* and another eight before Darwin was willing to state any conclusions, even tentative ones. All through these 18 years he worked on what he called "my theory," dealing at the same time with his own theological past and the alternative explanations that his contemporaries presented as explanations for changes in life forms. Increasingly he felt he had to discount the idea that God was micromanaging every detail of life. The long process of concluding that changes in living things were mainly due to natural causes rather than supernatural ones left many fine statements of his thinking. They show how a scientist deals with complexity. One of his statements included the following: "I am inclined to look at everything as resulting from designed laws with details, whether good or bad, left to the working out of what we may call chance, not that this notion at all satisfies me." Fundamentalists today, in their ignorance of scientific methodology, have treated that statement as an indication of doubt regarding his theory of evolution. The long delay in putting his theory into final form and his sensitive and humble approach to his colleagues in the course of his research provide an excellent example of a scientist at work.

The Introduction mentioned that America has a long history of exposure to good science teaching through the work of John Dewey. The methods he employed in the classroom are the same ones used by scientists in their research. They consist of a five-stage sequence of investigations and they always begin with a problem question for which there is no solution. The problem arises from experience, either within the ordinary course of living or as something that emerges from more deliberate study. The second stage begins with a guess or two, what scientists call hypothesizing. This second stage is vital. A hypothesis gives direction to the third stage, the search for relevant information via people, books, or experiments to help solve the problem. Without the guideline provided by an initial guess, a person can waste a lot of time in the search for information. The more serious part of scientific work comes with stage four when the information collected is compared with the initial guess. Often the first hypothesis has to be rejected because the information shows it to be false. An experimenter then has to come up with another hypothesis and try again. It is here, as mentioned previously, that fundamentalists so often misunderstand the nature of modern science. They think of it as discovering firm answers. The reality of modern science is that it constantly looks at discoveries to see what can be rejected. It is only when one hypothesis survives attempts to reject it, again and again, that it is given validation. That validation always remains open to rejection at a later time as fresh discoveries are made. If one examines the following short extract from Darwin's introduction to *The Origin of Species*, some of these stages of scientific research can be seen.

> When on board *HMS Beagle* as naturalist I was much struck with certain facts in the distribution of the organic beings inhabiting South America, and in the geological relations of the present to the past inhabitants of that continent. These facts, as will be seen in the later chapters of this volume, seemed to throw some light on the origin of species, that mystery of mysteries as it has been called by one of our greatest philosophers. On my return home it occurred to me, in 1837, that something might perhaps be made out on this question by patiently accumulating and reflecting on all sorts of facts which could possibly have any bearing on it. After five years of work I allowed myself to speculate on the subject, and drew up some short notes; these I enlarged in 1844 into a sketch of the conclusions which then seemed to me to be probable. From that period to the present day I have steadily pursued the same object. I hope that I may be excused for entering on these personal details as I give them to show that I have not been hasty in coming to a decision.

The problem that launched Darwin's extraordinary search for the forces that transform the appearances and functions of living things began in the course of the voyage. It is clearly stated in his first sentence. The second sentence reveals the hypothesis that began to take shape at an early point in the five-year voyage, namely that there is a common force or influence at work that might connect all life forms. It is clear from his words at this stage that he was unwilling to go beyond a very general type of hypothesis. There was a good reason for being tentative. Darwin had come on this exploratory trip around South America with some fixed ideas about life forms. They were based on his upbringing, especially on the teachings of his church. These teachings tended to explain all conditions of life in terms of the direct action of God. Darwin was now observing forms of life that seemed to be caused by the interactions of different physical environments. He realized at once that he needed to conduct extensive investigations in order to test the validity of his new and quite revolutionary hypothesis. Sentences three and four of the above introduction describe this third stage of the scientific method. He mentions arriving at a tentative conclusion in 1844. That was more than 12 years after his first awareness of the problem. It took him another 15 years of searching, consulting with colleagues, and conducting research on different forms of life before his work was published in 1859. Some of the details of that period follow.

Theory of Evolution

From his tentative conclusions in 1844, Darwin continued the quest for a mechanism that would encompass all the changes that take place from species to species. He found it in the writings of Thomas Malthus, whom he had met in London after returning from the *Beagle* and with whose book, *Essay on the Principle of Population*, he became familiar. He read it again in 1838 because Malthus' reasoning had become a strong rationale in his mind in support of his thesis. It carried a lot of examples from farm life, already quite familiar to him. Malthus' concluded that any crowded habitat of organisms would experience a filtering effect whereby the weakest would perish and he implied that this was God's way of preventing humans from getting lazy. Darwin saw in it the possibility of a seamless process of change from one form of life to another over very long periods of time. The great age of the earth that his friend Lyell had established was a necessary condition for this process. By 1856 he was busy compiling a massive book that would cover all of his thinking over the previous 20 years. Charles Lyell urged him to publish and not wait to do a comprehensive volume that would cover everything. Two years later, in the summer of 1858, he was shocked into action when he received a letter and manuscript from Alfred Russell Wallace who was in New Guinea. Wallace's 4,000-word manuscript contained a summary statement of the same theory as Darwin's.

Wallace was a naturalist 14 years younger than Darwin. He was not very well known in Europe because he had lived for most of his adult years either in Latin America or in Asia. While Wallace was laid aside in New Guinea, sick from malaria, Wallace reflected again on Malthus, whose ideas were familiar to him from his earlier reading. There were the familiar conclusions from that reading that those best fitted to survive would live on and the others die. The idea of the survival of the fittest, the same idea and from the same source that had shaped Darwin's thinking, struck Wallace afresh as the key to survival over time. He began to write and the manuscript that arrived in Darwin's mailbox weeks later was the result. Wallace had met Darwin once, in London, and knew thereby of his interests and history. Later, in 1857, they wrote to each other and Darwin explained that his many years of study were coming to an end and he hoped to publish by 1859. It is easy to see how big a shock it must have been for

Darwin to see his ideas in print by another scholar just as he was about to publish his. To make matters worse, just as he was wondering what to do with Wallace's manuscript, Darwin's family was hit with scarlet fever and his infant son died.

Darwin knew all along that someone might come out with a statement about biological evolution that would pre-empt his publication and he recognized that he could do nothing about such an eventuality. There had been widespread sharing of information for many years as is normal in good scientific circles. Darwin had shared his thinking for years with many colleagues. Now it seemed that his whole lifework was about to be scooped by Wallace. In true gentlemanly and scholarly fashion Darwin said to Lyell that he would rather burn his book than give the impression that he behaved in a poor spirit in the face of a competing publication. Lyell suggested that Darwin's earlier memo of 1844 and Wallace's be presented together at the next meeting of the Linnean Society so that the community of scholars could judge on the merits of each. These two papers were presented to the Society in the year that Wallace's manuscript arrived and fortunately for Darwin the limited coverage in both manuscripts left the members of Linnean rather indifferent to their content. Many scholars had already presented brief manuscripts on the ongoing search to explain changes in life forms. It was a very different story a year later when Darwin's thoroughly-argued book came out, *The Origin of Species: The Preservation of Favored Races in the Struggle for Life*, a volume of more than 150,000 words. Interest in it exploded like a bomb all over Europe.

Initially, in the years after 1859, opinion was divided among both scientists and religious leaders. Some scientists rejected it on religious grounds and some religious leaders readily accepted it. In general it was more widely received in Europe than in America. A number of scientists felt that there were insufficient numbers of fossils available to give credence to the theory. Alongside that objection lay the uncertainty of the age of the earth. Most scientists, including Darwin, knew that an enormous amount of time was needed to enable the known natural forces to effect change on emerging life forms. Lyell had greatly advanced knowledge of the age of the earth but Lord Kelvin, Britain's most important physicist, said in 1862 that the earth was no older than 400 million years. This uncertainty had to remain unresolved until radiometric dating methods, years after Darwin's death, determined the age as more than four billion. With the limited knowledge of his time Darwin had to envisage the operation of natural selection in terms of the competition resulting from the impacts of wind, rain, rocks, availability of food, temperature, and numbers of partners of the opposite sex to ensure continuity of life forms into the next generation.

Darwin's attachment to Lamarck's claim that an animal could transmit to the next generation characteristics acquired in its lifetime did not help. It had been long discredited but Darwin remained convinced of its truth for the rest of his life. In 1870 George Mivart, a professor of natural history, presented a number of objections to the mechanism of natural selection that were so persuasive that Darwin—always the scientist ready to reassess any theory—accepted the criticisms and modified the next edition of *Origin of Species* accordingly. He wrote at the same time that he had probably attached too much importance to the action of natural selection. Four more revisions of his book followed in later years, each revised with the same care Darwin had always given to his work. Unfortunately, the fact that Darwin had felt it necessary to do so many revisions gave rise to new criticisms. Modern scientific thinking was still at any early stage of development and many did not appreciate the fundamentals of testing and challenging research findings until there are no more valid objections. The influence of Malthus led to the subtitle for Darwin's book, subsequently referred to as natural selection. It was here, in his choice of the mechanism involved in evolution, that most differences of opinion arose with biologists, differences that remain at the present time. The element of genius lay in the idea of continuous change in living things from species to species over time. This was the heart of Darwin's thesis and it has stood firm and is today universally accepted as a valid scientific theory.

Evolutionary Mechanisms

Most of the objections to Darwin's theory came from disagreements over the mechanism Darwin had chosen, natural selection, even though Darwin had acknowledged at the beginning that there might be other mechanisms. As one looks back on these early reactions to Darwin's work two things become quite clear. First, Darwin had nothing to say about the origin of life. He accepted the traditional view that a creator was responsible for that and confined himself to what happened next. The other point is the perplexing behavior of creationists and IDs. They knew from the beginning that Darwin's thesis had nothing to do with the origin of life yet they continued to say that it does. It is hard to believe that this kind of thinking comes from serious thought. So much has been written on all aspects of Darwin's work that interested scientists and others could hardly miss them. One likely conclusion is that the real reason for the complaints from creationists and IDs about the origin of life is a reluctance to accept data that interfere with medieval interpretations of the Bible. Problems relating to this aspect of life will be examined in Chapter 6. For further discussion of mechanisms, one needs to look at a number of things, all of them continuing subjects of research at the present time. They include investigations into the factors that cause change, the speed at which they occur, and the directions they take from one species to another. The discovery of DNA in the 1950s, illustrated on page 14, was the culminating confirmation for the validity of Darwin's thesis. No longer could its basic tenets be questioned because human genes, stamped so clearly in every inch of the body, can be linked to similar genes in living things as far back as the most ancient fossils discovered to date.

Completion of the Genome Project, 50 years after the discovery of the structure of DNA, was another major milestone in evolutionary history when the entire human genome was mapped with every one of the three billion sequences identified and recorded for posterity. It involved a huge investment of time and money and it was recognized nationally in the United States and all over world as the greatest enterprise of the last decade of the twentieth century. Its story was told in a book, appropriately titled, *The Common Thread*, because it was a definition of the life of every human. It was also a resource made available to anyone and everyone so that advances could be made and are now being made in gene therapy. It's a library with code letters that carry all the instructions necessary for building and maintaining human life. Within every cell in the human body there is the information needed to make an entire human being. Chapter 7 shows how this new aspect of evolution is helping scientists as they seek to ameliorate the human condition. As research went on into the pace of evolutionary change, researchers discovered that there were huge gaps in the historical record. Sometimes in the past there were hundreds of millions of years for which no one has yet found any fossils. The reason for this may be that earthquakes or volcanic actions or even hits from asteroids may have destroyed life for long stretches of time. Until more is known about this, the quest for answers remains. Stephen Jay Gould, America's well-known expert on evolution, proposed a theory of punctuated evolution, implying that all evolution developed by a sequence of starts and stops. Unfortunately, Gould linked this theory to social evolution, a distortion that will be examined in the next section of this chapter.

Despite his mistaken reference to social evolution, Gould's claim that changes in living things came in starts and stops is strongly supported by recent research. More and more paleontologists agree that different forms of life persist over long periods of time virtually unchanged in form and function. Then, with some species, a change happens almost instantaneously. This is not today's meaning of "instantaneously." A sudden change in biological history may mean over 50,000 or 100,000 years. One example of change was taken from marine bivalves, creatures that look like clams and that had lived between 140 and 180 million years ago. For one period of approximately 10 million years they showed no change, then within the following one million years they were replaced with a very different new species. It is important to keep this aspect of evolution clearly in mind when human evolution is discussed. For decades in the twentieth century, there were old wives tales about humans developing from apes within a relatively short period of time. Darwin's weakness about mechanisms tended to support this error because he wrote about species as resembling branches of a tree, each branch being an extension from a previous species. Nowadays, with the science of cladistics so well advanced, we have more questions than answers about the sequences followed in the course of evolution. Cladistics is the branch of biological science that studies biological sequences.

These two of the three main aspects of mechanisms, pace and direction, continue to throw new light on the past as more and more fossils are discovered and the new field of molecular biology reveals the complexity of cells and genes. Enthusiasts like Richard Dawkins tend to overstate the powerful influence of genes, attributing to them the power to completely control both evolution and human and animal behavior. His books *The Selfish Gene* and *The Blind Watchmaker* give complete support to Darwin's mechanism of natural selection via random events even though almost all modern research in biology rejects that explanation. Random natural selection is one factor for life changes over time but by no means the only one. Dawkins made the same mistake as Gould by taking one bit of evidence and extending its application beyond the evidence. (Dawkins goes even further by asserting that there is no factual basis for belief in the existence of God—it can be said of him that he lacks intellectual humility, a characteristic that was an outstanding feature of Darwin's mind.) Mutational changes in human and animal cells, that is to say random changes in the numbers and types of genes being passed on to succeeding generations, are far from being random in their long term effects. They may be neutral or negative and lead to genetic drift that ends up with the total elimination of valuable traits. The basic notion of evolutionary advantage in random gene changes over time is not defensible.

The third major category of evolutionary mechanisms, what factors cause change, has many answers and many philosophies. Some of them have been included in the section "Before Darwin." Here this book is indebted to Simon Conway Morris, the distinguished professor of evolutionary paleobiology at the University of Cambridge, for one idea that is found in his books *The Crucible of Creation* and *Life's Solutions*. It is, like all great and revolutionary ideas, a very simple one. Animals think. They face problems and tackle them, usually in order to survive, and as they do they change. This is much more than just an idea because Conway Morris has extensive experimental evidence to support the claim that animals think. He focuses the different outcomes in the term "convergence." In essence this term says that there is a limit to the number of random options available, a limit to the most efficient forms of organisms in particular environments, and a limit to the number of ways of doing anything. The result is an evolution toward the predictable future form and function of an organism, a result that most biologists readily recognize but seem slow to explain. Accordingly the natural world is full of examples of animals thinking and acting. One of the most recent, now employed in hospitals regularly, is a dog's ability to identify a certain form of cancer before doctors can.

Conway Morris' approach is to study the history of animals just as people study human history. People never think of their lives, their families, their communities or their country as being the results of totally random causes. Events that happen are seen as beneficial or problematic. If the latter, then action is required to deal with whatever is encountered. The question that too few ask is why do people not apply the same logic to other forms of life? Why do people think that human experience is unique? Think more generally about experience worldwide, not just at the personal level. See how societies organize their lives even when they are widely separated from one another and there is no communication between them as was the case a few hundred years ago. They establish rules for behavior, property rights are recognized, and ethical codes emerge. There are consequences laid out if people break these social rules. Cannot other forms of life do likewise? The answer is that they do and the evidence is available to confirm it. The forms that emerge over time among different species of animals tend to be similar in different parts of the world, quite independently of one another. They learn because they think and interact over problems and imitate what they see in other communities.

If one takes the findings from brain research over the past decade or two, it can be shown that the automatic reactions by the brain to external threats have not changed very much in thousands of years. Reactions to present day events are therefore often the same even though the circumstances are totally different. Reaction to a threat of fear, for example, triggers flows of chemicals away from normal brain functions into strengthening muscles and accelerating blood clotting. Brain responses are the same if the external threat is a lion attack or an angry face. What is the best way to learn anything? Again brain research shows clearly that the answer is problem solving. When humans are confronted with relevant and manageable problems the brain is structured to find solutions and it operates best when this is the task needing resolution. Similarly, different groups of organisms solve the problems that confront them, usually issues of survival, by problem solving. Substantial experimental data, mainly fossils, are now on hand to confirm these things. Life forms that existed long before there was a *homo sapiens* discovered this mode of learning and survived. As research continues into how evolutionary processes occur it is likely that new, detailed understandings of the thinking processes of animals will give us the best clues to solving the uniqueness of human evolution.

Non-Darwinian Interpretations

This book previously mentioned the unfortunate comments of Gould in connection with his theory of punctuated evolution. Gould had been a strong supporter of communism although he disapproved of the way it had worked out in Russia, but he felt that its origin was due to the inevitable clashes that must come from time to time in society. In his mind, just as bursts of life arrive from time to time in nature, so too to bursts of freedom come to humans, again and again, when they revolt against bad masters. This was a totally unjustified interpretation of Darwin's theory concerning biological evolution and it gave support to others in Europe who created parallel theories that extended all the way from nature worship to the development of human societies. In much the same way, Karl Marx was the first to make wrong use of Darwin's theory. He saw it as support for his own ideas about class struggles in society. Because he saw this struggle as something that happens naturally and inevitably, he jumped at the opportunity of exploiting Darwin's thinking since it enabled him to compare capitalists and workers with animals competing with one another in order to survive. The tragedy of Marx, as contrasted with others who misappropriated Darwin's work, is that it led to a world-wide disaster that lasted for 70 years.

Ernst Haeckel, a German zoologist, linked Darwin's theory to mystical philosophies so that it applied to almost anything. He saw evolution as a general thing affecting all aspects of life, not just biological. Where Darwin was clear that his theory had nothing to do with the origin of life, Haeckel boldly declared that there was no God and that everything related to the origins of life were natural events. Like Lamarck and others before him, Haeckel envisioned evolution as synonymous with progress. He saw the whole range of human knowledge as pointing to greater and better phases of development. He even hinted at national achievements in his native Germany that would lead to a superior type of human. The result was that evolution, in Germany, for a long time meant anti–God materialism and changes in human society. There is no indication that Haeckel's thinking affected Hitler despite the similarities. Similar thinking to that of Haeckel came from another German, Wilhelm Bolsche, but he interpreted the theory of evolution as leading to cooperation and harmony. He acknowledged the brutal side of natural events but considered them to be transitional, paving the way to a better future. Both Haeckel and Bolsche wrote major works. These were translated into English and widely distributed.

Herbert Spencer was a British philosopher who wrote extensively and who used the word "evolution" or its meaning in every one of his publications. We need to remember that the word "evolution" in England in the nineteenth century had a different meaning that it has today. At that time it meant change toward a desirable end, and it may be that Spencer did not think deeply enough about the central idea in Darwin's theory of evolution. At least he studied Darwin enough to come up with the phrase "survival of the fittest," a phrase that Darwin used in a subsequent edition of his book. Spencer's view of life was that everything and everyone moved toward better and better conditions. He applied the idea of evolution to society and wrote about it moving toward happier and happier times. His ideas were extremely popular both in England and in America. Both of these countries were in the heyday of industrialization and they were sure that it would bring wealth and happiness. Spencer also applied his utopian ideas to other things. He saw the Rockefeller empire as better than the corner store and a human as better than an amoeba. When he came to America in 1882, the year of Darwin's death, his books were bestsellers and he was greeted as a hero. Darwin had little use for Spencer's writings. He described them as having no scientific value.

Darwin died in 1882 and was buried in Westminister Abbey.

2

Identifying American Christian Fundamentalism Today

Fundamentalism differs from traditionalism or orthodoxy in that it is a movement opposing any disruption of those traditions and orthodoxies.

—Nancy T. Ammerman,
Fundamentalisms Observed, 1991

Fundamentalism is a word that was a defining term for evangelicals in the 1800s. As the word is understood today, one needs to look back to a more recent series of events at the beginning of the twentieth century. Between 1909 and 1915 evangelical theologians from Britain, the United States, and some other English-speaking countries produced a series of books in order to reassert fundamentalist beliefs in opposition to challenges from biblical criticism and Darwin's theory of evolution. The details of these fundamentalist beliefs are listed in Appendix A and they will be examined and discussed later. At the heart of all of them is a defense of biblical infallibility. For the long 2,000 years of Christianity, right up to the early years of the nineteenth century there were no serious threats to infallibility, nor was there much reference to it. It was just assumed that the Bible was to be trusted, every word of it. It would not be out of line to describe it as a book that was seen as given by God, untouched by human hands, or written by people who acted as secretaries for God. There were many past interpretations of the Bible but none of them affected the prevailing certainty over the Bible's inerrancy and infallibility. The concerns about biblical criticism and evolution had their roots in fundamentalist opposition to modern science. This was due in part to ignorance about the nature of science but it was also due to the influence of shrill religious voices from people who believed, wrongfully, that scientists are opposed to belief in God.

One of the early fundamentalists was a British theologian, John Nelson Darby (1800–1882), who had left the Anglican Church to form a new group of Christians that came to be known as the Plymouth Brethren because of the location where much of their early development occurred. Darby introduced a new outlook on future events, a form of millenarianism in which a secret rapture of Christians is predicted as part of an unfolding sequence of events called dispensationalism. Darby's influence across the U.S. was extensive from 1830 onwards and, when the books known as *The Fundamentals* were written, Darby's dispensationalism was prominent in them. His ideas were popularized by C. I. Scofield in his annotated Scofield Bible, published in 1909. Scofield was one of the authors of *The Fundamentals*. Ernest R. Sandeen, in his book, *The Roots of Fundamentalism*, claims that the Darby movement was an integral part of the fundamentalist movement from its beginning. If one looks at the Christian literature of recent years, there is substantial evidence to support Sandeen's claim. Dispensationalist ideas seem to be very much alive. Tim La Haye and others have succeeded in publishing millions of successful Christian novels based on Darby's idea of a secret rapture of Christians. A scene in one of these novels has all the novelty of a best seller. The captain of an airplane who happens to be a Christian is suddenly and silently raptured and the passengers and crew are left with the problem of what to do. The book is appropriately titled *Left Behind*.

Evolution of Fundamentalism, 1870 to the Present

Fundamentalism as a worldwide concept was thoroughly researched by Martin E. Marty and R. Scott and published in several volumes under the title *Fundamentalisms Observed* by the University of Chicago Press in 1991. The epigraph at the head of this chapter is taken from their chapter "North American Protestant Fundamentalism," contributed by Nancy T. Ammerman. It is an accurate description of American evangelical fundamentalism today and it is important to note in it the emphasis on resistance to change. It is this refusal at the present time to deal rationally with the findings of modern science that distinguishes American evangelical fundamentalists from other evangelicals. Ammerman goes on to say that fundamentalists can be found today either waiting for the rapture, a reference to the continuing influence of Darby, Scofield and their successors, or actively lobbying the White House, the political action aspect of fundamentalism that is most visible today. She goes on to show that there are many subgroups, each with its own distinctive features, but overall most of them would identify themselves as evangelicals and they are generally opposed to biblical criticism and evolution. For over a century they persistently attacked these two modern developments, not at a constant rate but rather in three major buildups of activities, each caused by particular sets of events that raised the ire of fundamentalists at the time and inspired extraordinary efforts.

The first buildup became evident in the last quarter of the nineteenth century. It was a time when science was still understood as being the same as its sixteenth century predecessor. It consisted of looking at the world and the Bible without the influence of the reader's opinions and experiences or those of others. One writer, in the 1790s, expressed it in words like the following: "I like biblical theology that does not begin with a hypothesis and then warps the facts. I like the Baconian system in which facts are collected from either nature or the Bible and general laws deduced from them." The name Baconian relates to Sir Francis Bacon, one of the scientists who pioneered new thinking about 400 years ago when science was still in its infancy. The Baconian style of science did not inject into the study of the Bible anything that was not visibly there so it reinforced the traditional mode of Bible study. All that was asked of the reader was the ability to read and then to deduce general laws from what was read. It was when theological scholars began to utilize the skills of modern science that fundamentalists became concerned and opposed them. They rejected all suggestions that what you see, and what you think you understand, are affected by your past experiences and biases. There was no division among evangelicals in 1870. Every evangelical was a fundamentalist and vice versa and all of them opposed modern science.

The second buildup occurred in the first quarter of the twentieth century and was focused in the series of books known as *The Fundamentals*. It was a time when enormous changes were affecting national life. More than 12 million immigrants arrived from Europe between 1900 and 1916 and soon afterward America was launched into World War One. Industrialization and urban life were transforming traditional lifestyles. These and other changes created social tensions. When Russia became a communist nation in 1917, many people were convinced that its godless philosophy was the direct result of evolution. Some influential writers, unfortunately, had said so in their writings. Partly as a result of this kind of thinking, and partly because the theory of evolution was not yet understood, the focus of opposition to modern science shifted to evolution. It was seen as the principal cause of all social evils. Some even coined a word for it, "evil-ution." For the years that followed World War One, state after state banned the teaching of evolution in schools. William Jennings Bryan, a national political leader, led the campaign against evolution. It culminated in the famous Scopes trial of 1925 in Dayton, Tennessee, with an unexpected outcome. This trial proved to be the catalyst that divided evangelicals into two groups. Forever afterward there would be evangelical fundamentalists and evangelical non-fundamentalists.

Some scholars, including Ammerman, point to Jerry Falwell's Moral Majority and the political actions associated with it in the 1980s as being the third build up. Certainly the development of the Moral Majority was a powerful influence in society and it marked a high point of success for fundamentalists. However, the beginning of this third phase was not in the 1980s. Twenty years earlier, a new course called The Biological Sciences Curriculum Study (BSCS) was introduced to schools all across the United States. It was focused on evolution as the key organizing idea for the whole course and this infuriated fundamentalists. They felt that their efforts over the previous decades against evolution had been a failure. Beginning in the 1960s and continuing for the rest of the century and right up to the present time, a continuous series of organizations and publications emerged, all of them dedicated to the prevention of the teaching of evolution in schools. These organizations carried different names. At first there was creationism, then creation science, and now intelligent design. This last one, in order to gain the support of political leaders, claimed that it was a scientific organization, not a religious one. The scale of opposition was immense and extensive from the 1960s on. Other countries became involved at different times. Now, as can

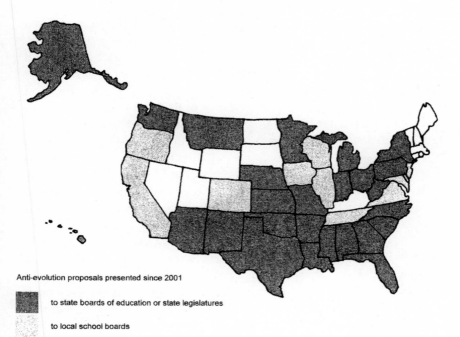

Anti-evolution proposals presented since 2001

to state boards of education or state legislatures

to local school boards

This map shows the locations of anti-evolution proposals presented since 2001, evidence of widespread opposition.

be seen in the figure above, there is no indication of abatement in this mindless assault against modern science.

Opposition to Evolution

There is a paradoxical history to the assault on modern science because, for all of the eighteenth century and much of the nineteenth, the emerging field of science was popular and every new discovery was welcomed. Furthermore, at the time of American independence, there was a bond of unity between evangelical Christians and the political leaders of the new country as both made use of the old form of science. It was the science of Newton, they would say, one of the greatest scientists of all time, and therefore the right one to use. Sometimes it was called Baconian and sometimes Scottish common sense science. These older forms of science are fully acceptable among fundamentalists. The thing they cannot accept is modern science with its hypotheses and theories. Memories of the Christian character of America at the time of independence frequently became a measure of the ideal society, and they still do, leading to the emergence of restoration societies dedicated to putting America back to where it was in 1776. The other tradition that has deep roots in America is related to the great revivals of the past two centuries. They shaped cultural norms and even tended to suggest that intellectual efforts were unnecessary. D. L. Moody's emphasis on conversion certainly gave the impression that thought at any deeper level was superfluous. He would urge his friends to focus on faith. Make sure that the sinner knows what he has to do and make sure that he does it. It is interesting that one of Moody's closest associates, R. A. Torrey, was one of the main organizers of *The Fundamentals*.

The crisis that emerged in the 1960s at Wheaton College illustrates the kinds of tensions about evolution that are commonplace today and keep surfacing all across the nation. Wheaton was an extremely significant location for the events that occurred there more than 40 years ago and were telecast as an historical documentary on the PBS network in 2005. Unlike so many of the Christian colleges that emerged from Bible school origins in the twentieth century, Wheaton dates back to the 1860s. It had strong ties to the evangelist D. L. Moody (1837–1899) who has often been called the "Father of Fundamentalism" because of his devotion to Biblical infallibility, pre millennialism of the kind that Scofield and others had advocated, and the holiness movements. All three of these Christian emphases were dominant features of Wheaton College in the late 1930s and were strong at the time of the 1960s event. R. A. Torrey (1856–1928) was a close friend of Moody and he was one of the key organizers of *The Fundamentals*. Torrey had close ties with Wheaton when he was superintendent of Moody's Bible Institute prior to becoming president of the Bible Institute of Los Angeles. There were other links too that made Wheaton a fundamentalist touchstone for the twentieth century.

Charles Blanchard was president of Wheaton College from 1877 to 1925. His tenure therefore covered a critical period of fundamentalist opposition to modernism. Blanchard was a friend of D. L. Moody and like Moody he supported premillennialism and holiness teaching. He had dreams of restoring the morality that had peaked at the time of American independence, based as it was on the Scottish common sense science. The question that troubled Charles

Blanchard was this: if, according to common sense science, every individual is endowed with both the moral and rational sense to do what is right, how could such large numbers of Americans turn away from God. He concluded that the twentieth century had become an age of insanity. It is easy to see from all of this history why Wheaton had deeply imbedded opposition to all forms of modernism and why it remained ready to do battle against them in the 1960s, at a time as it happened when modernist ideas burst afresh on schools in the form of a new curriculum on evolution. This development will be considered further in Chapter 5.

In the last quarter of the twentieth century, two of Wheaton's graduates became very well known. One was Carl Henry, founder of the journal *Christianity Today*, now the unofficial organ of evangelical America. It celebrated its fiftieth anniversary in 2004 when it could readily claim to be the most widely read evangelical journal in the country. Billy Graham was the other graduate of fame. Both in America and worldwide, fundamentalists justifiably regarded him as their leader because he quoted from the Bible as his authority but without the embellishments of infallibility and inerrancy, or the emphasis of premillennialism, all of which still defined fundamentalism. Perhaps the most interesting link of all in modern times was the emergence of a scholarly publication from a faculty member of Wheaton College, a publication that helped define for the foreseeable future the difference between evangelical fundamentalists and other evangelicals. These other evangelicals are referred to as nonfundamentalist evangelicals, or NF, within this book. The Wheaton book, a thoughtful and well-documented publication, is Mark A. Noll's *The Scandal of the Evangelical Mind*. This book supports the position of evangelicals who accept such findings of modern science as the theory of evolution. By implication, since Christian colleges usually have one statement of faith for all faculty members, it probably identified many other contemporary members of Wheaton's faculty.

This is a long digression from the events at Wheaton College in the 1960s but it will be a valuable reference when differences between NFs and the others are discussed. The crisis that developed began with a visit to the college by Walter Hearn, presumably as a visiting scholar, because soon after his departure the college faculty was required to sign an edited statement of faith that would prevent any recurrence of his views. Some faculty members considered them to be heretical.

Hearn assured the college and its students that Darwin's theory of evolution was in no way an attack on belief in God. It dealt only, he assured them, with what biologists are discovering about nature. There were immediate reactions to Hearn's visit and parents called in to find out if the college had gone liberal. Students reacted with such comments as "evolution is hard to accept," or "we don't know much about evolution," and faculty members sought to assure them that Hearn was wrong. At the college's assembly they sang a song with the following lyrics: "I don't believe in evolution, I know creation's true, Adam is my ancestor and not a chimpanzee." Kenneth Ham, director of the "Answers in Genesis" organization, was invited to speak to the college. He is well known as one who reads the Bible literally, that is to say, with today's meanings in the words. He assured the students that day means day in Genesis just as it means day for us.

The PBS documentary of 2005 went on to interview students from high schools, other colleges and universities to find out their thinking at the present time. In many instances little had changed over the 40 years. Even in non–Christian institutions the interviewer was met with opposition to evolution, often because young people were unwilling to consider that humans may have come from non-human ancestors. At one high school a group of students, presumably inspired by parental encouragement, presented a petition to the local school board requesting that intelligent design, the latest form of anti-evolutionary protest, be included in their science curricula. Forty years after Hearn's visit, Keith Miller, a geologist from Kansas, visited Wheaton. Miller had been busy trying to cope with extremist views in his own state where all references to evolution and an old earth were once removed from school texts and where there was discussion about doing it again. Miller's reception at Wheaton was polite and uneventful and many students were still unwilling to accept Darwin's theory of evolution. The whole story of Wheaton's reaction to evolution in the 1960s is critical to an understanding of the present scene. It was in the 1960s, for reasons that will be explained later, that a new anti-evolution campaign was launched by fundamentalists in order to prevent, if they could, the use in schools of a high school biology course known as BSCS.

Evangelicalism

Evangelicalism in Britain dates from the early 1700s as a movement found in both old and new churches and not identified uniquely with any one of them. David Bebbington, in *Evangelicalism in Modern Britain: A History from the 1730s to the 1980s*, defines evangelical churches as the ones that emerged in the wake of the Protestant reformations of the sixteenth and seventeenth centuries. He uses the biblical phrase, "new wine that has been poured into many bottles," to identify them. It took time for the new name to gain wide acceptance because "evangelical" meant "people who belonged to the gospel" and there was fear that its use might suggest that others did not belong to the gospel. By the close of the eighteenth century the term was in common use. One magazine, *The Evangelical Magazine*, was launched in 1793 to assist those dedicated to spreading the gospel and this kind of outreach activity soon became one of the clearest distinguishing features of the new movement. Bishop Ryle of Liverpool, who later contributed a chapter to Volume Nine of *The Fundamentals*, pointed out that it was not the distinctiveness of their doctrines that marked out evangelicals from others but the emphases they gave to a few doctrines. These emphases became the hallmark of evangelicalism, establishing it as a distinct tradition.

Bebbington provides a simple anecdote from the beginning of the nineteenth century to introduce what he considered to be the four foundational characteristics of evangelicals. A member of the Anglican Church remembered how, in his childhood days, evangelicals used to divide humanity into two groups with the approved half being those with a converted character, who helped people in need, read their Bibles, and held strongly to the doctrine of the cross. These four features, according to Bebbington, had become consistent features of evangelicalism. He named them as conversionism, Biblicism, activism, and crucicentrism. One needs to examine these four pillars of evangelicalism in some detail to see how they were understood in the nineteenth century before evolution and higher criticism became the chief concern of fundamentalists. While all four pillars remained as the defining features of evangelicalism throughout the nineteenth century, different emphases appeared from time to time among the various Christian communities. Of special interest because of the events that unfolded at the beginning of the twentieth century was the dominance of biblical authority. Again and again in the 1800s and continuing up to the present time, leading evangelicals insisted that no aspect of Christian faith was more important than biblical supremacy.

Conversionism meant personal choice and justification by faith alone, without any human merit. In the late nineteenth century its experience was a very different event when compared with Billy Graham's present day campaigns where decisions for Christ so often seem as matter of fact as joining a club. Bebbington provided an example of a conversion which he said was typical of that time: a young man kneeled down once he was alone, determined not to get up until he was assured that his sins were forgiven and he had received peace with God. In the course of this activity he cried repeatedly as he asked God for forgiveness. The passage of time was ignored as he continued to wrestle with God. The young man could not remember how long he had been praying. Finally there was freedom from fear and guilt and he knew that his sins had been forgiven. Orthodox teaching affirmed that conversions like this one were strictly the work of the Holy Spirit in response to faith but enthusiasts at times employed various modes of persuasion to secure conversions. Public proclamation of the gospel was the chief method of securing converts and the design of these public meetings often utilized crowd psychology to encourage individual decisions. Major revivalists like Charles Finney gave considerable attention to the techniques needed to ensure mass conversions.

The evident transformations in the lives of these nineteenth-century converts convinced everyone that a major change had occurred. They would work harder than before, save money, and be ready to help a neighbor. Some used language that was quite explicit to identify them, saying that it marked the boundary between a Christian and a pagan. It was not long before a clash with their Book of Common Prayer arose among Anglicans. It was the only major nineteenth-century theological issue that arose among evangelicals but it was a big one and it was never adequately resolved. In the Anglican order, for baptism, a child is declared to be regenerate at the end of the ceremony, although clearly no decision was made by the child and there was no decision about conversion. This was heresy to evangelicals. It was an example of a problem that will be discussed later when this book looks at biblical interpretations, conflicts between personal or group convictions and the dogma of Christian institutions. J. B. Sumner, an Anglican leader who later became Archbishop of Canterbury, proposed a compromise to solve the disagreement between the evangelicals and the Anglican Church. He said that baptismal regeneration meant something less than becoming a Christian.

He did not define what it did mean, nor did he change the wording in the order for baptism, so the probl em persisted and is still present today.

Activism first consisted of efforts to secure the conversion of others and it found expression in a variety of activities by individuals, churches and evangelical publications, each geared to securing more conversions. The missionary movement of the nineteenth century and the first half of the twentieth century were dramatic expressions of the same evangelical activism. In the 1880s there were the extraordinary commitments of the Cambridge Seven, who were outstanding athletes and scholars and who chose to surrender their future to take up missionary work in China. Exceptional examples like these galvanized many others to launch out into missions in Africa, Asia, and South America. It was the time of European empires and evangelicals felt drawn to share the gospel with people in the colonies. A number of missionary societies sprang up to coordinate these extensive missionary activities. Activism was equally evident socially. Britain was in the heyday of industrialization and conditions in the overcrowded cities were deplorable. Many evangelicals took up the cause of providing better health and sanitation for workers in the cities.

Biblicism, third on Bebbington's list, was central to the life of every evangelical and every church. One bishop said that the absolute supremacy assigned to Holy Scripture is the first principle of the evangelical religion. His statement came in the context of discussions over the place of either reason or church authority. At other times there were similar discussions over the place of the priesthood and the sacraments and, again, there was consensus on biblical authority being supreme. Overall, evangelical loyalty to the Bible implied giving top priority to the following over all other authorities: the direct contact of the individual with God the Father, the freedom and sovereignty of the Holy Spirit, and the place of God the Son as the sole high priest for humans. There was general agreement on biblical inspiration and reliability, but until the beginning of the eighteenth century there was no particular definition or even emphasis on infallibility and inerrancy. These attributes came into intense use much later in that century. It seems clear now that doctrines about the Bible were rare before 1800. It was a book to be read literally and one on which to reflect. There were generally fluid views about the nature of inspiration.

Crucicentrism provided a vivid point of reference for evangelicals because it carried a visible symbol, the vertical and horizontal lines of the cross, seen almost everywhere today in churches and Christian organizations. Belief in a substitutionary atonement because of the cross was always the heart of evangelical convictions. Furthermore it became the dominant motive for spiritual growth. Holiness movements sprang from the cross and they subsequently represented a substantial part of evangelicalism. Nothing in the life of Jesus made any sense apart from his resurrection, an event that was poorly understood in the early church despite claims for historical evidence. There was nothing in any of the first century Mediterranean cultures that could be compared with Jesus after his resurrection. The effect of that event however became the inspiration that led to the extraordinary spread of Christianity. N. T. Wright, in *The Resurrection of the Son of God*, lists the varied explanations that have been given. The resurrection was the main focus for the New Testament writers and it eclipsed the significance of the incarnation.

Contemporary Evangelicalism

While these observations on evangelicalism relate to Britain, the interactions across the Atlantic made them equally valid for America, and until 1925 there was little to distinguish evangelical fundamentalists from NFs. Their total numbers grew rapidly in the twentieth century so that by the 1970s and 1980s they constituted a third of the U.S. population. By the 1990s that figure had risen to a half. These calculations were obtained through Gallup polls and the one thing that Gallup used to identify people was this question, "Do you describe yourself as a born again or evangelical Christian?" As I have already pointed out, the doctrinal positions among evangelicals is generally the same for NFs and others. The following are their agreed statements of belief, but conflicts inevitably arise when loyalty to their statements of belief clashes with new knowledge, just as it happens in Christian institutions:

1. The 66 canonical books of the Bible as originally written were inspired of God, hence free from error. They constitute the only infallible guide in faith and practice;

2. There is one God, the Creator and Preserver of all things, infinite in being and perfection. He exists eternally in three Persons,

the Father, The Son, and the Holy Spirit, who are of one substance and equal in power and glory;

3. God created Adam and Eve in his own image. By disobedience, they fell from their sinless estate through the temptation by Satan. This fall plunged humanity into a state of sin and spiritual death, and brought upon the entire race the sentence of eternal death. From this condition we can be saved only by the grace of God, through faith, on the basis of the work of Christ, and by the agency of the Holy Spirit;

4. The eternal pre-existent Son became incarnate without human father, by being born of the Virgin Mary. Thus, in the Lord Jesus Christ, divine and human natures were united in one Person, both natures being whole, perfect, and distinct. To effect salvation, he lived a sinless life and died on the cross as the sinner's substitute, shedding his blood for the remission of sins. On the third day he rose from the dead in the body which had been laid in the tomb. He ascended to the right hand of the Father, where he performs the ministry of intercession. He shall come again, personally and visibly, to complete his saving work and to consummate the eternal plan of God;

5. The Holy Spirit is the third Person of the Triune God. He applies to man the work of Christ. By justification and adoption we are given a right standing before God. By regeneration, sanctification, and glorification our nature is renewed;

6. When we have turned to God in penitent faith in the Lord Jesus Christ, we are accountable to God for living a life separated from sin and characterized by the fruit of the Spirit. It is our responsibility to contribute by word and deed to the universal spread of the Gospel;

7. At the end of the age, the bodies of the dead shall be raised. The righteous shall enter into full possession of eternal bliss in the presence of God, and the wicked shall be condemned to eternal death.

J. I. Packer, a leader among NFs, wrote in *Fundamentalism and the Word of God* that, since God is the author both of nature and of the Bible, true science and a right interpretation of the Bible cannot conflict. He went on to add that evangelicals would continue loyal to the evidence both of the Bible and empirical inquiry, resolved to do justice to all the facts from both sources. Unfortunately he then went on to attribute to nineteenth century liberals the most extraordinary interpretations of Darwin's theory of evolution, suggesting that liberals tried to use it to remodel Christian doctrines. Any scholar who tried today to distort, in this way, such a well-known and well-respected scientific theory as Darwin's would soon be laughed out of court. Packer must have known the theory of evolution. This is the kind of behavior seen when attempts are made to defend Biblical interpretations that are clearly repudiated by factual evidence from nontheological sources.

Evangelical scholars who are competent in both science and theology know that human destiny was not determined by the behavior of one human pair in the past, despite the assertions in the evangelical statement of faith. Instead, unlike the above statement of faith regarding Adam and Eve, they see possible outcomes from the ancient past that do not violate either science or the Bible. They recognize that there is a problem with human nature. Humankind participates in strange and harmful things. While this is true, no responsible scientist can believe that these problems are due to one disastrous act in the past by two people. At most, one could say, struggles developed in hominid lines as they evolved into *homo sapiens*. As they discovered their dependence on their creator, coupled with an awareness of a creator, a challenge came with that discovery. It raised the question of whether they would recognize their dependency on their creator or, alternatively, turn away from the creator to find sufficiency in themselves. Thus human autonomy was asserted over creaturely dependence and succeeding generations of humans chose the same course.

Uncertain Unity Between Fundamentalists and Other Evangelicals

From time to time throughout the twentieth century, attempts were made to reestablish the old unity between the two dominant branches of evangelicalism. Publication of *The Fundamentals* was the first effort in this direction but, after the debacle associated with the Scopes trial, tensions rose again. For most of the 1920s, it seemed that fundamentalism had received a fatal blow, but gradually over the succeeding two decades a large number of independent publications kept it alive. Many of these were related to the worldwide missionary movement which had reached a high point of activity in the interwar period. However, a much more powerful ally emerged within North

America, the network of Bible schools and Bible institutes. These places developed their own linkages through conferences, publications, and training centers. One publication from Texas, *The Fundamentalist*, had a circulation of 35,000 in 1941. A year later the strength of fundamentalism induced the New England Fellowship of Evangelicals to launch a "National Conference for United Action among Evangelicals." From it came the "National Association of Evangelicals" which united the two branches of evangelicalism in a loose association for the rest of the century. The distinctiveness of fundamentalism seemed to have been absorbed in the new unity, and expressed in the public ministry of people like Billy Graham, but it was to reemerge later in a much stronger form.

Many journals and media outlets try to define the things that separate fundamentalists from other evangelicals today because the latter are anxious to establish their identity, especially to make clear that they are not tied to old literalist views of the Bible. It is not easy to clarify the differences because the two groups have statements of faith that are almost identical. Critics say that, if there is an important difference, why doesn't each side state clearly what it is, using words that anyone can understand? Take, for examples, two important issues in national life, opposition to abortion and the theory of evolution. Gallup and other polls consistently show that the majority of Americans support this double opposition. Does this mean that most Americans are fundamentalists? Surely this cannot be so! Other differences need to be found. NF people claim that they use their minds when reading their Bibles and do not just accept everything they read as if it carried today's meanings in every word. This distinction is strongly asserted in Britain, and ever since the emergence of U.S. movements such as the moral majority, British NFs have found it necessary to restate the meaning of fundamentalism.

Essentials: A Liberal-Evangelical Dialogue, a 1988 publication by John Stott, the well-known Anglican NF, states that evangelicals were loyal to such historical doctrines as the following that were included in *The Fundamentals*: (1) biblical authority and the deity, (2) virgin birth, (3) atoning death, and (4) bodily resurrection of Jesus. Stott added that the writers intended to affirm the fundamentals of the faith in opposition to modernism but, unfortunately, words change their meanings and today there are fundamentalists whose mindset can be identified in one or more of the following eight statements: (1) a general suspicion of scholarship and science, at times degenerating into anti-intellectualism; (2) a mechanical or dictation view of biblical inspiration with a consequent denial of the human, cultural element in the Bible and therefore the need for biblical criticism; (3) a naïve, almost superstitious reverence for the King James version of the Bible as if it were quasi-inspired; (4) a literalistic interpretation of the Bible, leading to insufficient recognition of poetry, metaphor, and symbol; (5) a separatist ecclesiology; (6) a cultural imprisonment, including prejudice and prosperity teaching; (7) a denial of the social implications of the gospel; (8) an insistence on premillennial eschatology and an uncritical espousal of Zionism. Not all of these are found in American fundamentalism but they form a valuable benchmark for distinguishing NFs from others.

Does fundamentalism mean in North America that they value highly the possibility of Christians achieving significant political power and enacting laws based on the Bible? Despite the fact that this would be a violation of the separation of church and state, the answer is that both fundamentalists and NF people hold this value. Again and again, there is evidence that the majority of Americans want their political leaders to be Christians and as such to make decisions based on biblical values. Where does this idea come from? It is a relic of medieval times when the church held political power and ruthlessly destroyed anyone who opposed it, somewhat like dictatorships of the present time? While anyone, evangelical or otherwise, has every right to aspire to be president, governmental action must be based on the well-known principles of democracy, which mean that minority rights are as important as those of the majority. Johan Heyns, moderator of the Dutch Reformed Church of South Africa, once said "We never again want to have temporal power because we made such a mess of it when we had it." This view is entirely in keeping with the repeated emphasis found in the New Testament that the role of the Christian community is to be the conscience of society, influencing it from within, not controlling it through political power.

It is in the desire to see biblical values determine decisions at the highest levels of government, a desire common to both groups, that paradoxically show the clearest differences between fundamentalists and NF people. The former are opposed to so many of the things they see in American society that they tend to be isolated from its mainstream life. While they are vocal, as part of Jerry Falwell's moral majority, with large followings through agencies like television evangelists, somehow they do not identify with everyday life. NFs, while disapproving of many things in society, are deeply involved in it, identify with it, and therefore are better equipped to reach the highest levels of political power. They happily sing the battle hymns of the republic, endorse warfare, and are completely at home with the stock market and globalism. Yet, despite these major differences in lifestyles, NFs and fundamentalists are united in opposition to many aspects of science, especially to the theory of evolution. They think that it is anti–Bible and anti–God. What is the reason for this outlook?

The answer lies in a widespread reluctance among evangelicals to come to terms with what some evangelicals rightly know, namely that "all truth" is "God's truth." NFs who have risen to the tops of their fields in science and are engaged in research at the frontiers maintain a sort of schizophrenic mindset toward the relations between different kinds of knowledge, especially where they seem to conflict. It could be caricatured in a man who goes to church on Sunday and hears sermons on God's creation of the universe in six days of 24 hours each, then on Monday, as he leaves memories of Sunday behind him, he continues his biological research into the trilobites of the 500-million-year-old Cambrian Explosion. Thus it is easy to see why fundamentalists and NFs find common ground in their opposition to the theory of evolution. The lack of strong advocacy by scholarly NFs of the value of this foundational paradigm for biological research leaves the field open to those who say that evolution is opposed to God and the Bible. They dominate the television media every Sunday morning and they encourage individuals and groups to get directly involved in the political process. It is now commonplace to see people campaigning for biblical values to guide all congressional and presidential decisions.

Week by week in the halls of Congress in Washington, DC, and in neighboring locations, evangelical organizations arrange meetings with elected members and their staffs to study the Bible. They seek guidance from it on how to cope with decisions they have to make in such areas as taxation, foreign aid, cloning, and trade. One of these organizations is the "Center for Christian Statesmanship," launched by the Rev. D. James Kennedy of Coral Ridge Presbyterian Church in Fort Lauderdale, Florida. Kennedy's weekly telecasts reach three and a half million Americans, more than the number that received copies of the publications of *The Fundamentals* in the early years of the twentieth century. As a result, the Center for Christian Statesmanship gets a lot of attention in Washington. Elected members of Congress are very attentive to an organization that is supported by millions of voters. The organization Americans United for Separation of Church and State argue that America must not turn the holy scriptures of one group of people into public policy. Kennedy's organization's response is that if candidates stand for what they believe is God's will for America and voters elect them, then is it not all right for a biblical worldview to be imposed on every American? Is this outlook a recipe for an American theocracy? Could it happen? Is it right for candidates to go to voters with some other person's or some book's view, rather than their own, of what is right for America?

Fundamentalists as the Moral Majority

Concerns about morality are so deep among fundamentalists that the phrase "The Moral Majority (MM)" has often been used as a synonym for them. MMs see themselves as a nonpartisan political organization to promote morality in public life and to combat legislation that favors the legalization of immorality. As a political organization they differ from some fundamentalists who do not want to be involved in political action but in all other respects there is little difference between the two groups. Jerry Falwell in *The Fundamentalist Phenomenon* identifies five positions that are at the heart of MM. They are as follows: (1) Pro-life. Life begins at fertilization. Abortion is characterized as a biological holocaust, and is strongly opposed; (2) Pro traditional family, that is the legal marriage of one man and one woman. Homosexual and common-law marriages should not be accepted and no special rights should be given to them; (3) Opposition to illegal drug traffic. All legal means should be employed to stop it; (4) Pornography is opposed. All efforts short of censorship should be made to stop this poisonous tide; (5) The State of Israel and Jewish people everywhere are supported. This is an essential commitment of MM. No anti–Semitic influence is allowed in MM. Some preliminary observations on two of these positions, zygotes and support for Israel, follow here.

MM insists that it is not a political party and it is not a religious organization. It says it neither endorses candidates nor seeks to elect born-again ones but it supports those who are in accord with its stated positions. Furthermore it assures everyone that it is committed to work within the nation's multi-party system, to support civil rights, and to recognize that those who do not agree with its convictions are in no sense an immoral minority. MM feels it represents the majority of Americans, a position that fundamentalists also take. MM is working through every media agency, through groups and individuals, and using its economic influence in the marketplace to bring America back to moral sanity. If MM, as it claims, represents the majority of Americans and its views were to become national policy there are big problems with some of its positions, despite all the disclaimers that have been enunciated. To state that human life begins once a zygote appears may be a fine statement of faith, the kind that Roman Catholics would affirm, but one that has no factual support. There are no identifiable human characteristics in a zygote. Some would assert that because there is the possibility of a human in it therefore it is a human but possibilities of being a human occur in many places.

Support for Jewish people because of the benefits it brings to Americans, based on a literal interpretation of the twelfth chapter of Genesis, represents an inadequate understanding of the original text as will be shown when Biblical interpretation is addressed in Chapter 6. Identifying such support with a national state today, one that is a member of the United Nations and has a responsibility toward all the other nations of the world, and to assert that opposition to Israel is the same as opposing God, is absurd. MM's position with regard to Israel goes on to say, in Falwell's *The Fundamental Phenomenon*, that both human history and MM's interpretation of the Bible provide solid evidence that God deals positively or negatively with the nations of the world on the basis of their dealings with Israel. There is no responsible historian alive today who would support such an outrageous suggestion. One can suppose that most of the world's nations never had occasion to take a position of support for or opposition to the State of Israel. Falwell's statement on support for Israel gets even more confusing when he outlines the national boundaries of that country as a specific area of land that God supports. His support of Israel brings Falwell completely in line with Lyman Stewart's thinking. He was the man who financed the publications of *The Fundamentals*, and who said on one occasion, "Any man who does not have a grasp of dispensational truth cannot possibly rightly divide the word of truth."

Stewart not only supported dispensational truth, including strong support of Jews. He paid for the republication of William Blackstone's book, *Jesus Is Coming*, at the beginning of the twentieth century. Blackstone's book, with the help he received from Stewart, was translated into 42 languages, including Hebrew. More than half a million copies were sold. Blackstone was written up in the *Encyclopedia Judaica* as an early Christian Zionist. When Jews were persecuted in Russia, Blackstone launched a conference in order to restate the importance for Americans of Jewish welfare and presented to the United States president a memorial from that conference. In one of his talks, Blackstone said, "The return of the Jewish people to their own land would precede the coming of Christ to earth." He often said that if people wanted to know their place in God's chronology, all they needed to do was look at Israel. It was Blackstone's and Stewart's dispensationalist-premillennialist view of the world that Falwell had picked up to support his drive for political action. It was a view of the world that had persisted for a century and is still held today by many. The repeated claim of fundamentalists that they do not get involved in politics is blatantly contradicted by this long-standing devotion to support for Israel. Nothing today is more political than Israel.

The inadequate grasp by MM of both the content and methodology in present scientific work has parallels in the positions that fundamentalists take on abortion and stem cells. Everyone would like to avoid abortions whenever possible without violating women's rights. No one advocates abortions as a desirable medical practice. However, the fundamentalists who strongly try to stop abortions are quite supportive of capital punishment. Do not both of these constitute the deliberate taking of human lives? International research has thoroughly researched the effectiveness or otherwise of capital punishment as a deterrent to murder and they have found out, contrary to Jerry Falwell's assertion, that removal of capital punishment makes no difference to the numbers of murders in any given place or time. Why are fundamentalists not campaigning against capital punishment as strongly as they oppose abortion? The practice of in vitro fertilization is another area in which fundamentalists have problems. Jerry Falwell asks, "what rights do the unselected embryos have?" This extreme view of the sanctity and uniqueness of the physical aspect of human DNA is taken independently of information that relates directly to humans. For example, there is no recognition of the fact that humans and chimps share more than 95 percent of their DNA sequences.

It was in the emergence of the Moral Majority in the early 1980s that fundamentalists secured the political power they sought. The ways in which it happened are closely related to Jerry Falwell's initiative. He gave fresh impetus to the distinctiveness of fundamentalism as he launched his moral crusade. The old differences between NFs and others resurfaced because now evangelicals had to choose between their traditional role of seeking to influence society from within rather than, like the members of the Center for Christian Statesmanship, trying to control it through political power—a bold declaration of intent to move evangelical fundamentalists into the public arena in order to formulate a non-partisan political organization. Its goal would be to promote morality in public life and to combat legislation that favored the legalization of immorality. Falwell identified with the doctrinal positions of the fundamentalists from the beginning of the twentieth century but, unfortunately, in his enthusiasm to establish the uniqueness of American fundamentalism, strayed here and there from historical accuracy. There was indeed uniqueness in Falwell's action, not in the theological beliefs of the participants, but in the switch to political activism and in the tidal wave of evangelical conservatism that ensued.

Falwell's first moves came in the form of a series of sermons dealing with the danger of what he called pietism, the tendency of Christians to withdraw from society and concentrate on spiritual activities within their own groups. His definition of pietism was not correct but it served the purpose of changing the prevailing outlook. It was not an easy message to convey and still more difficult to accept. His church members had listened for years to condemnations of the evils of American society and the need to rescue people from that world in order to bring them into the safety and nourishment of Christian fellowship in fundamentalist churches. Falwell had to maintain that view of life while, at the same time, opening up an altogether new perspective on how and why the rescue mission had to be done differently. Pietism, he pointed out, was unhealthy because it hid people from the real world and, furthermore, it was an inadequate understanding of the Bible's depiction of Christian living. Having raised the question of a healthier interpretation of normal biblical lifestyles, Falwell and his team of preachers had to fill in the gaps and build the model of fundamentalist behavior that would be ready for the exodus out of pietism. Sermon after sermon had a single focus but numerous rays of light pointing toward new thinking. The Christian life must never be seen as partly spiritual and partly unspiritual. Life is one whole reality and every bit of it is sacred. The pastor, the bus driver, the doctor, the student are each called to Christian ministry. There is no spiritual value in being a pastor rather than a car salesman. The only thing that matters is what a person is equipped for.

So, week by week, sometimes through the voices of visiting speakers, Falwell's fundamentalist troops were prepared for the public arena. It took time because there were deeply imbedded notions of how fundamentalist Christians should behave in order to stay clear of the bad society around them. The following were typical of the comments from preachers, all of them designed to create a new identification with the world around them. Life was divided into two categories with the pietists, the spiritual and the unspiritual (or to use the language of today, the worldly and the Christian) but none of this is found in the Bible. The good and the bad are there with no separation. The moment people begin to think of society as being in two parts, they give priority to one, the Christian or the spiritual part, and treat those in the other part as second-class citizens. The result is that the Christian feels like an outsider in society and society ignores him or her simply because there is no common ground, no mutual interests, no shared values. If one person goes to a Bible school to train for work in a church and another trains to be a doctor, which one of the two is in the better position to influence societal decisions about abortion? Many Christians behaved as if on an island, building big walls around the island to keep out the bad world. They can't shut out the whole world and they shouldn't try. They must be real and live out their lives in the real world. They ought to forget their code language, their sense of superiority, and their separatism.

Once the mindset of separation had been transformed into an exodus, Falwell was ready to expand the membership base. While still emphasizing biblical infallibility and inerrancy to his fundamentalist colleagues, he urged evangelicals and all sorts of others to join the Moral Majority. He appealed for support to make the Moral Majority effective, enabling as many as possible to get involved in the political process and the social life of the country in order to reach the whole person for the cause of Christ. At the same time there were changes at Falwell's home base, Thomas Road Baptist Church, to bring it into line with the new public involvement. A number of social agencies were added and Liberty Baptist College, the liberal arts college that had been attached to the Baptist Church, became Liberty University with graduate and professional programs that were designed to send professionals into all areas of society. The next step required the articulation of a clear rationale for the work of the Moral Majority. Most of the people involved had been committed to the premillennial rapture, the quiet disappearance of Christians from the earth prior to all sorts of troubles occurring. Their outlook prior to the emergence of the Moral Majority had been withdrawal from world events except for careful observations of developments in order to discern the signs of the cataclysmic events that would usher in the end of the age. Falwell had to contend with this outlook.

He found it in one uncertainty among the various fixed predictions. It related to the period before the rapture when God would judge Christians, not the Jews for whom troubles were to come later after the rapture. Falwell focused on this pre-rapture space of time and presented it as a window of opportunity that had no fixed prophecy associated with it. If American Christians became active in restoring good living during this period they and the nation would be preserved. The great tribulation, as the prophecy was called, would inevitably come but, if American Christians were to go all out as it were and get involved in electing political leaders to reflect biblical morality in domestic and foreign policies, the nation might retain its freedom and the work of the gospel might be completed. Falwell urged his Moral Majority to help with registering voters and taking a stand whenever and wherever moral values are threatened. By so doing there would be revival and the restoration of morality. There would also be freedom, said Falwell, to complete the evangelization of the world in one generation and thus take a multitude to heaven when the rapture comes.

Television was the heart of communication in the 1980s. The computer world and the internet were still in their infancy. The voices of the televangelists could reach every home and they did. One and a half billion dollars a year were spent on television ministries in the

1980s and their impact in support of the Moral Majority was enormous. Then, within a short period of time, sex scandal after sex scandal began to appear among these television missionaries. By the late 1980s it seemed that televangelism had collapsed, reminding many of the disastrous collapse of fundamentalism in the wake of the Scopes trial of 1925. Paradoxically, the very opposite happened. The media love scandals, especially ones related to religion, so the scandals came into the glare of the daily news and stayed there for years. Thus, by a series of events that were the opposite of all that Falwell intended, The goal of the Moral Majority to be involved in the life of the nation and to be seen in that capacity had been achieved. The political scene of America in the 1980s and 1990s, however it may be interpreted by historians in the future, bears convincing evidence of the power of Falwell's Moral Majority to effect it.

Late in 2005 came the devastation of New Orleans from a powerful hurricane. The death toll was large, approaching 1,000, and floods damaged or destroyed an enormous percentage of the area's homes. This level of destruction from natural causes had not been seen in the continental United States for a very long time, so it was not long before premillennial Christians began to link the event with the pre-rapture tribulation of Christians about which Falwell had spoken. Could it be that this was a punishment from God for the decline of morality in New Orleans and could it be reversed if the lives of people in that city were reformed and they began to work for national renewal? No one was willing to say that God had deliberately punished the city because of their low morality but one report from Falwell's Liberty University came very close to the new theology of the Moral Majority. Franklin Graham, son of evangelist Billy Graham, spoke at Super Conference 2005, organized by Falwell's Thomas Road Baptist Church at Liberty University. This was part of his talk:

"There is satanic worship and sexual perversion in New Orleans and God is going to use the storm to bring revival. God has a plan. God has a purpose. I have prayed with clergy in New Orleans for deliverance from this dark spiritual cloud and I see signs of promise as Christians work to restore the city."

On the same day that Graham was talking about God's plans for revival in New Orleans, Bill Moyers of PBS and CBS was giving a very different message about the hurricane to New York's Union Theological Seminary. He discounted the idea that God was in any way responsible for the hurricane but acknowledged that millions of conservative Christians saw it as a punishment from God just like Noah's flood in the past. To Moyers this was an irresponsible way of reading and interpreting the Bible. He then went on to attack what he saw as a political holy war by conservative Christian activists, a sectarian crusade for political power. He compared their activity to the sorts of things that occur in Muslim nations that are theocracies, where religion and state power are in the same hands. In his talk Moyers said that the Republican Party is already a theocracy and there is a danger that the country could become a theocracy too. The possibility of the country drifting into a theocracy is an important theme for discussion and debate and the fact that it is being publicly faced is the best guarantee that it will never happen.

Fundamentalism in Private Schools

Across America today and growing in number year by year is a network of fundamentalist Christian schools. They have about a million students in all, not a big percentage of the nation's total, but a very significant number if one considers the enormous influence that can be exercised by a few people when they are in the right place at the right time. The closest parallel to describe a typical fundamentalist Christian school is the military. It's a place of total involvement, a place that decides your behavior at all times of the day and night, and it's a place where you are under authority with consequences that follow every infraction of rules. Here is how the head of one of these schools talked about his educational goals:

> We feel we are wasting time if we teach a young person all day, then he goes out and leads his own life. If we're just touching academics we do not care to have such a student. We run a 24 hour school, we link with homes and churches, so that we can deal with the moral aspects of life and influence a student's total behavior. Typically in our school students are here Friday and Saturday evenings. They are also here on Wednesday nights and on Sunday for church. Ours is an authoritarian point of view. We require the students to stay within God's structures and God's system of order. All of our teachers are Christians. There are no exceptions. In such a setting students are influenced by invariant models of correct belief and right behavior.

One only needs to read part of the network's statement of faith to confirm that all of their schools have the same doctrinal position as fundamentalists:

> We believe that the Bible, both the old and new testaments, was verbally inspired by God, and is inerrant and is our only rule in matters of faith and practice. We believe in creation, not evolution; that man was created by the direct act of God and in the image of God. We believe that Adam and Eve, in yielding to the temptation of Satan, became fallen creatures. We believe that all men are born in sin. We believe in the Incarnation, the Virgin Birth, and the Deity of our Lord and Savior Jesus Christ. We believe in the vicarious and substitutional atonement for the sins of mankind by the shedding of his blood on the cross. We believe in the resurrection of his body from the tomb.

The departures from the statement of evangelical faith are important: the theory of evolution is attacked, a serious difference because it says that a particular biblical interpretation, not the Bible itself, is the authority that governs Christian lives. The emphasis on man in creation rather than man and woman, or Adam and Eve, fits the bias that is evident in the schools, namely that men are the authority figures in the Christian home and women are to be obedient to them.

In every way these schools reflect the old goal of fundamentalism before Jerry Falwell decided to switch it into political activism. Withdrawal from the world because of its evil ways was the outlook of the old fundamentalism and the outlook of the people who first launched the American Association of Christian Schools (AACS) in 1972. They saw society as sliding downward in a floodtide of socialistic and communistic legislation and decided that private Christian schools must be started to stem this tide of evil. They spoke of the public schools as brain washing, socialistic, amoral, and atheistic institutions. The leaders of AACS would often affirm that teachers in Christian schools understand that their students are neither aware of their own hearts nor what is good for them. Like all of humanity they are depraved, born with a sin nature. They need no help to do wrong but they must be taught how to do right. This extreme view of human behavior, coupled as it always was with dire warnings about the evils in our liberal, humanistic world, cleared the way for imposing a new lifestyle. There was little demand for thinking and plenty of demand for obedience and conformity. These have always been the demands of fundamentalism. They inhibit innovation and reinforce the status quo.

3

Opposing Biblical Criticism, 1865 to 1900

Critics say that the Bible is not verbally inspired but the line can never be drawn between the thoughts of God and the words of Scripture.

—L.W. Munhall, Vol. 7,
The Fundamentals

When it comes to criticisms from fundamentalists, two things dominate, the higher criticism of the Bible and Darwin's theory of evolution. The second one will be examined in Chapter 4, the first one in this chapter. Biblical or higher criticism features in each of the first three volumes of *The Fundamentals* and in a dozen more chapters among the other nine volumes. Sometimes it is a general criticism of any record and any one person's writings in which the Bible is not seen as historically accurate. At other times the critique is specific, delineating all the objections, as in the chapter in volume eight by W. H. Griffith Thomas of Toronto, Canada. This is how he introduces his chapter on Old Testament Criticism and New Testament Christianity:

"Re the Old Testament, it is now being taught that the patriarchs of Jewish history are not historic persons; that the records connected with Moses and the giving of the law on Sinai are unhistorical; that the story of the tabernacle in the wilderness is a fabricated history of the time of the exile; that the prophets cannot be relied on in their references to the ancient history of their own people or in their predictions of the future; that the writers of the New Testament, who assuredly believed in the records of the Old Testament, were mistaken in the historical value they assigned to those records; that our Lord himself, in his repeated references to the Scriptures of his own nation, and in his assumption of the Divine authority of those Scriptures, and of the reality of the great names they record, was only thinking and speaking as an ordinary Jew of his day, and was as liable to error in matters of history and of criticism as any of them were."

Thomas emphasizes the role of the supernatural in any assessment of Old Testament history. While, like other contributors to *The Fundamentals*, he welcomes the value of critical investigations into the circumstances surrounding Old Testament events, he feels that the anti-historical higher criticisms have no place for supernatural happenings. This may well have been the outlook he encountered in the publications he studied but it is not inherent in the modern approach to history. There are always records of past occurrences for which no explanation can be found and so they are relegated to a kind of mystery category. It is entirely improper to expect historians to deal with supernatural explanations of things. Convictions of that kind belong to faith, not fact, and historians should and do limit their findings to what can be factually established. There is a much bigger question involved when referring to ancient documents as historical or otherwise. People tend to put the present-day meaning into this word and it may have nothing to do with whether or not something happened. This is a general problem whenever documents like the Old Testament are under study. Not only are questions about historicity raised. Relevance to present scientific knowledge, potential errors in language translations, and problems in knowing the original meanings of the languages employed all feature in discussions of documentary reliability. The cuneiform illustration on page 65 is a reminder of the folly of asserting the infallibility of, say, the cuneiform records of early Genesis, compounded as they are with numerous parallel accounts from non–Jewish sources. It is equally foolish to imply verbal infallibility, despite Munhall's reference above, if no one has ever seen the original words.

Many of the fundamental truths of historic Christianity are not involved in the higher criticism because no discoveries to date relate to them. They were and are unrelated to science so fundamentalists ignored them. There are exceptions to this general statement. James Orr in the first article in Volume One of *The Fundamentals* describes

The earliest form of writing in Mesopotamia was cuneiform, wedge-shaped indentations made on soft clay before it hardened.

one of these exceptions in his chapter on "The Virgin Birth of Christ." He said that the higher critics call it a fable. Here, as in the discussion about rejecting anything supernatural, one runs into a basic misunderstanding. The narrative about the virgin birth in a society like the Jewish one of 2,000 years ago, if it were true, would not be generally known or talked about until a considerable amount of time had elapsed. Very few outside the immediate family circle would know about it. If it were shared beyond the immediate family, alternative accounts would soon get into circulation and the family would be shamed. Furthermore, few would believe what they were told. So, on the one hand, the higher critics say it never happened because there is very little mention of it in the New Testament. If it were as important as Christians say it is, they add, surely we would find it referred to in many places all through the New Testament. These considerations sometimes illustrate a weakness in the arguments employed by some higher critics. Just like fundamentalists who fail to deal ration-ally with biblical criticism, higher critics, at times, fail to present their arguments in ways that can be defended rationally.

The first five books of the Old Testament, known as the Penta-teuch, are the most frequent targets of criticism. It is here that the higher critics have good supporting evidence. Their focus of criticism is almost always directed toward authorship and date. In Volume One of *The Fundamentals* in Chapter Six, Dyson Hague first identifies his difficulty with modern science, which will be dealt with later in this chapter, before he summarizes one group's findings regarding the Pen-tateuch:

> It is a fundamental truth in philosophical and scientific inquiries that no regard whatever should be paid to the conjectures and hypotheses of thinkers. Consider instead the axiom of the great Newton himself and his famous words, " I do not frame hypotheses." It is notorious that some of the most learned German thinkers are men who lack in a singular degree the faculty of common sense and knowledge of human nature. Like many physical scientists they are so preoccupied with a theory that their conclu-sions seem to the average mind curiously warped.

Here in a nutshell is the consistent view of science among fun-damentalists, stick to the scientific methods of the 1600s, the science of Newton's time, and have nothing to do with any of the things that were discovered since that time. Dyson, in Chapter Six, goes on to summarize the group's criticisms of the Pentateuch: "In their under-standing the Pentateuch consists of four completely different docu-ments, each composed at a different time by persons who had no contact with one another when they were writing." These documents are commonly known as J, E, D, and P, and they may have been assem-bled at any time between 700 and 400 BCE.

Hague continued his assessment of the group by saying that the scholars who were involved had a strong bias against the supernatu-ral, just as Thomas had about the higher critics in Volume Eight of *The Fundamentals*. It seems that the authors of these books had no place in their thinking, for the most part, of scholarly investigations that were independent of belief in the Bible. Such an outlook makes sense if one links this position with Hague's insistence that only the science of Newton's time is reliable. No person in Newton's time, and not for a thousand years before that time, conceived of scientific inves-tigations apart from belief in the Bible. Newton, despite his great achievements in science, always worked within the universal, Bible-believing, culture of his time. He studied the Bible every day, convinced that it was true in every detail, always expecting that his work would reinforce belief in the Bible. He spent more time on biblical research than on his scientific masterpiece, *Principia*. In one period in later life he made a special study of Solomon's Temple to try and find out the significance of its dimensions. It is difficult to understand why a man with Newton's scientific competence would do this. When a friend, Thomas Burnet, had difficulty fitting scientific findings to the general assumption that Noah's Flood covered the whole earth, Newton suggested that God probably arranged a special miracle to make it happen. This is precisely what fundamentalists do today to resolve similar conflicts.

Hague makes no attempt to refute the scholarship that proposed J, E, D, and P. Instead, he dismisses it all as unworthy of a considered reply. This was probably due to his presumption that nothing trustworthy could come from anyone who did not believe the Bible. Here are some of the things he wrote in response: "For some reason, and at some time, and in some way, someone, no one knows who, or why, or when, or where, wrote J. Then someone else, no one knows who, or why, or when, or where, wrote another document, which is now called E." This kind of writing continued in the same monotonous way until he had covered D and P as well as the various editors who might have been involved. The assumptions he made were that such writers had lived and had compiled these documents. It is unlikely that any evidence for the existence of such ever existed and certainly no reason to imply that the critics thought so. By the same token the critics could just as easily write the same list of maybes for those who claim documentary evidence for the traditional authorship. Later in his chapter, Hague continues his diatribe against the critics and the authors he claims they had found: "The critics allege that the four documents are internally inconsistent and undoubtedly incomplete. How far they are incomplete they do not agree. How much is missing and when, where, how, and by whom were the missing parts removed? Was it some thief who stole or copyist who tampered, or editor who falsified?"

There is no doubt that Hague had a lot of trouble with modern science. How would he have coped with Charles Darwin's very tentative initiatives when he first began to elaborate his theory? His statements were full of uncertainties. Nevertheless at the heart of all of them was a powerful concept, one that in time would become clear and revolutionize huge areas of scientific knowledge. Hague, presumably, would have mocked Darwin's work because it lacked the certainty and finality of biblical truth. He never seemed to think that maybe the origins of biblical material were multiple rather than the work of one person at one time. Maybe he was thinking of the ways that books and chapters are written in modern times. In earlier periods, information, even inspired information, was often passed on by word of mouth over long periods of time and perhaps recorded in some symbolic form. There were no copyright laws to limit the freedom of people to copy what they had heard or seen. The custodians of the history of a tribe or larger community would collect information from the past and, with improvements in language and materials on which to write, preserve the history of their people. Hague saw biblical truth as something delivered by an inspired and authorized messenger. This was how he concluded his observations on the critics: "If not Moses then who did write the books of Moses? If there were three or four, or six, or nine authorized original writers, then why could there not have been fourteen, or sixteen, or nineteen? Who were these original writers? How did they receive to write and who gave them that authority?"

This book has devoted a lot of time on Hague's chapter because its content is typical of all the chapters in *The Fundamentals* dealing with higher criticism. In his concluding paragraphs, Hague takes time to point out that he and the many others who hold traditional views of the Bible are not opposed to the pursuit of scientific investigation. He says that the only people he and others like him oppose are the biblical critics who are unbelievers. This is the repeated refrain of fundamentalists: return to seventeenth century science and the form of biblical beliefs of that time and all will be well; do not tell us about science that comes from unbelievers. All of the arguments mounted by the critics for the four sets of documents J, E, D, and P were based on the new science of text analysis. By comparing words, sentence structures, and colloquialisms, researchers can identify the parts of a text that have a distinctive character. Clearly, Hague did not recognize the existence of this or any other technique for dividing biblical documents into two or more originals. A different approach to Hague's was taken by two other authors of *The Fundamentals*, Franklin

Johnson in Volume Two and J. J. Reeve in Volume Three. Johnson introduced a mistaken interpretation of Darwin's theory to explain the history and literature of the Jewish people. He selected Herbert Spencer as the source of his evolutionary theory. He then included Darwin as someone who had given support to Spencer. It was a doubly mistaken interpretation of the original.

Johnson's approach was evidence of the carelessness with which evangelicals examined Darwin's theory of evolution at the time of *The Fundamentals*. They decided all too quickly that it was bad and so they tended to make mistakes when, later, they had occasion to assess it negatively. This book describes some of these mistakes in Chapter 4. Johnson's first mistake, a common one with fundamentalists, was to assume that Darwin's evolution was somehow related to the truth of the Bible. It is true that Johnson was commenting on the distortions of higher criticism as he saw them but he should have dealt with their misunderstandings about Darwin. It would have strengthened his refutation of the critics' position. Perhaps he was unable to do this. Spencer was one of those imaginative English writers who decided that Darwin's theory of evolution, which related only to biology, could be applied to all spheres of human endeavor. A lot of others who, like Spencer, knew little about evolution, also decided to apply it elsewhere. Professor Jordan, according to Johnson, was one of those higher critics who had envisioned the history of Israel and the documents of the Old Testament as one evolutionary process. Johnson gave no indication of the evidence that the critics advanced in support of this extremely generalized perspective on human history.

Central to the use of evolution by the higher critics in both Johnson's and Reeve's chapters is the meaning that the word carried in nineteenth century England. It stood for progress toward desirable ends, the opposite meaning that Darwin saw in his theory of evolution. To Darwin, everything was fortuitous, sometimes good, sometimes bad. That was why Darwin did not use the word "evolution" when he first outlined his theory. Spencer and others, with no supporting experimental evidence, thought it would be fine to use it in its English form and they discovered it was a popular idea, especially in America. Everybody likes to think that society is moving toward better days. Most of the higher critics, according to Reeve, base their conclusions on a similar kind of evolutionary hypothesis. This was how he defined it in his chapter:

It's a vision of a cosmos developing from the lowest types and stages upward through beast and man to higher and better man. Through the ages an increasing purpose runs, one God, one law, one element, and one far-off divine event to which the whole creation moves. All nature and history are the product of internal forces. There is no break in the chain of cause and effect, no miracle or anything supernatural, and hence no interference by God in the natural course of events. He is a prisoner in his own cosmos.

Reeve's summary assessment is an understatement: "I saw that the hypothesis did not apply to a great part of the world's phenomena."

This chapter began with a series of statements by Griffith Thomas from his contribution in Volume Eight of *The Fundamentals*, under the title "Old Testament Criticism and New Testament Christianity." Thomas listed some of the major features of higher criticism and with each one made it clear that he, as an evangelical, rejected them. Later he listed a number of the approaches to biblical study that he would regard as essential. His response list is a useful statement with which to finish this section. It provided a clear explanation of the evangelical position: the first requirement was a recognition of the supernatural element as the feature which distinguishes the Bible from all other books; the second was the recognition of the enlightened spiritual experience of Christians over the centuries past; the third was the recognition and acceptance of the general history and uniqueness of the Jewish people; lastly, Bible study must be in harmony with the views of Jesus' disciples regarding biblical authority. Before continuing with the study of modern science and its relation to the science of Newton's time, one needs to take note of the evolution of the higher criticism.

Evolution of the Higher Criticism

Higher criticism means criticism that calls in question the traditional assumptions about the history and the authorship of various parts of the Bible. As modern scientific techniques are applied to the Bible it is often found that traditional assumptions about the content conflict with new discoveries. The Fundamentalists' battle is with modern science because of this and only with modern science. As nineteenth century criticism developed it became clear that very little was known about the customs and languages of Mesopotamia, or Iraq as it is now called, the place associated with many of the biblical events. Over the years, new techniques were developed for dating documents, so researchers are now able to decipher with considerable accuracy the ancient records and artifacts from Iraq. Archeological research turned up thousands of cuneiform tablets like the one shown in Figure Three. To understand the meanings of these documents, scientists have to learn all they can from various sources of the customs and languages of the people who lived at the time these tablets were written. Everyday phrases that are colloquialisms rarely appear as part of written language but it is important to know them if one is to understand the culture within which they came. One example of this is the Biblical use of the number 40 to indicate a large amount. It seldom means what modern Americans mean by that number, just as modern Americans do not mean exactly one minute when they ask someone to wait a minute.

The role of oral tradition in Jewish history is very important. There are occasions in Jewish history when all the people were required to recite their laws on a regular basis in order to ensure accurate retention. One writer points out that there is almost no reference in the Old Testament to the existence of manuscripts before the time of the return from exile. Some written material may have existed but nothing approaching the volume seen in present Bibles. The same writer suggested that almost all of the written material in the first five or more books of modern Old Testaments were oral accounts until after the return from exile. There is always a temptation to think of oral history as being less reliable than written records because of the ways records are now kept. The truth about ancient history is that oral records are far more reliable than written ones for two reasons: written records from 3,000 years ago were not reliable and mistakes were common as now known from archeology; the materials on which events were recorded could easily be destroyed in the moist climates of Iraq and neighboring places.

Most of the scientists who are experts in the literature or the history of the lands of the Bible subscribe to the Document Hypothesis to explain the creation of the early part of the Old Testament. This hypothesis states that the content found in the first 10 books of modern Bibles came from several different sources and involved several people. The content was assembled over a long period of time. Putting it in summary terms, they say clearly that Moses never wrote the first five of these books. Various anachronisms that their research uncovered are provided as evidence for their positions. For example, the reference to Philistines and Abraham in Genesis 21:32–34 could not have happened. The Philistines did not arrive in Canaan until well after Abraham's time. Bruce Waltke, an expert on the history of the Old Testament, points out that anyone attempting to interpret the first two chapters of Genesis must first be thoroughly acquainted with the history of ancient Mesopotamia and equally familiar with modern science. He then adds his own view of these chapters. He says they are myths and quickly adds that that word meant something quite different in the ancient past compared with our interpretations of myths today. In the past that Waltke was investigating, myths were stories about God and his works among humans. They did not mean either "history" or "science" as is understood today.

Why is higher criticism a concern? This may at first seem like a meaningless question given that fundamentalists are committed to a trustworthy Bible, one that they believe is as reliable now as it was a thousand years ago. The reason this question is asked is because of the mounting evidence that large numbers of fundamentalists are biblically illiterate. They say they believe the Bible but how can that be true if they do not read it? This is a question that hangs over fundamentalists' heads as they campaign for biblical inerrancy. Polls reveal a great lack of knowledge of the Bible. Only half of the United States population can name as many as four of the Ten Commandments from the Old Testament and about the same number fail to name any one of the authors of the four gospels of the New Testament. Of even greater significance is a misguided conviction about the overall nature of Jesus' teaching. Three quarters of the nation's people say that the main emphasis in his teaching was similar to what we call the American dream, the idea that we can succeed if we make the effort. Ben Franklin's words for this outlook were, "God helps those who help themselves," and most Americans say it is part of what the Bible teaches. Could it be that what really matters to people is not what the Bible teaches but what they assume or they are told about its teaching? Whatever might be the reason for their opposition to higher criticism it is clear from their statements that most fundamentalists do not know what it is. They are just opposed to any and all changes in the long-standing, historical understandings of the Bible.

Modern science takes account of the way we approach new discoveries by looking at the backgrounds we bring to them. Michael Polanyi, the Oxford University professor who received a Nobel Prize in the middle of the twentieth century for his work on personal knowledge, was one of the people who changed our thinking about what used to be called objective science. He showed conclusively how an individual can be quite wrong about the things he observes we because his biases and interests affect how he sees them. It used to be thought that if one puts aside any ideas concerning the outcome of an experiment and stuck to the concrete, measurable results, the answer would be free from error and free from any human influence. This is no longer true. There is no such thing as pure objectivity in science so the only way to be accurate is to conduct numerous experiments by different people in different places until a clear consensus is reached. It is the same in biblical studies, perhaps even more important because few people are completely unaffected by what they already know about the Bible. The theologians who researched the literary and circumstantial details of the Old Testament, and found some of them to be different from what was thought, were not dealing with the truth or falseness of the Bible. They were reporting on some new discoveries that affected the traditional names that were assumed for authorship and the dates that had been given for the writing of the Old Testament, especially as these discoveries affected the Pentateuch.

Common Sense Science

The problem for fundamentalists was that their science, that of common sense, the one that introduced the modern phase of science in the seventeenth century, gave convincing support to the Bible that they had been using for a long time. They saw no benefit in the new science that was emerging in Germany and Britain. That science added uncertainty and complexity where none had previously been perceived and it introduced confusion to the frameworks of language on which so much prophecy had been constructed. In other words, the new science that featured in the higher criticism, whether conducted by evangelical theologians or others, was likely to destroy their infallible and inerrant Bible. The earlier nature of science, first defined by Francis Bacon and later developed by Thomas Reid of Aberdeen, Scotland, appeared to fundamentalists to be a fine support for an infallible Bible. Reid's ideas were easily shared with the United States as they took shape while America was still a British colony and it was easy for people to travel between the two places. It is because of their devotion to the older science that fundamentalists dislike the criticism and that they are anti-science. Henry Morris, the creationist who dominated the movement in the 1960s and 1970s, insisted that the words "science" and "knowledge" referred to the same thing and that the essence of the scientific method is experimentation and observation. Identical words are heard in 2005 from representatives of the new creation science museum in Kentucky. People are scientists, they say, observational scientists, the only reliable kind.

Thomas Reid (1710–1796), the founder of Common Sense Science, entered Aberdeen University at the age of 12 to study theology. Beginning university studies at that age seems extraordinary to us today but it was not so unusual in Scotland at that time. It was after he had completed his degree in theology and was appointed to a church nearby that Reid began to challenge the ideas of the leading philosophers. He was quite puzzled and upset when he read the words of the German philosopher Immanuel Kant (1724–1804), "to the extent that knowledge depends on the structure of the mind and not on the world, knowledge would have no connection to the world." To Reid, this sounded like nonsense. He was more upset and angry when he read the writings of his compatriot David Hume (1711–1776). Hume's book, A Treatise of Human Nature, included sentiments similar to those of Kant, namely that humankind's perceptions of the real world and the conclusions drawn from them are quite unreliable. Hume added that the same uncertainty applies to morality. Notions of right and wrong cannot be trusted. One has to rely on customs and traditions in order to understand the right morality. The double skepticism in Hume's book, the rejection of both morality and an ability to understand the world around us, became the inspiration to set Reid thinking in new directions.

Before continuing with Reid, one needs to consider some aspects of the context within which he wrote. Aberdeen University, the place where Reid established his theory of science and morality, celebrated in 1995 its 500th year of existence and one of the major articles in the publication associated with the celebrations described Reid and his work. The emphasis in the article was on Reid's view of morality, the principal but less understood part of his philosophy, and the related need for moral training. Inherent ideas of morality and rationality had been known for centuries before 1495 but it was Reid who gave them clarity and validity. Their restatement in the 1995 publication added strength to the original work: "It is not more evident that there is a real distinction between true and false in matters of speculation than that there is a real distinction between right and wrong in human conduct." Around the middle of the twentieth century C. S. Lewis in *The Abolition of Man* had earlier expressed support for Reid. Incidentally, loyalty to its medieval origins is still visible in Aberdeen University. The theology faculty can be found, physically, at the heart of the institution as the queen of sciences, its ancient name. The title of the 1995 publication, written in Latin, the *lingua franca* of 1495, carried the university's motto: "Where shall wisdom be found? The Fear of the Lord is the beginning of Wisdom."

Reid rejected outright the idea that the physical world was a mystery. To him it was a place where anyone with a normal intellect could make sound judgments about the things that are there just as a person could make sound moral judgments on the basis of an innate moral sense. Reid's ideas caught the attention of a wider public, including the university's administrators, and he was appointed to a teaching position there. He continued to promote his convictions that a firm grasp of truth can be obtained by observation. All it takes, he would assert, are eyes to see and ears to listen. In his mind the evidences from the senses, from memory, and from the relations among things that can readily be deduced are all quite clear. To oppose them would be foolish. They are the first principles of any philosophy and therefore can be summarized as common sense. His major book, *An Inquiry into the Human Mind on the Principles of Common Sense* (1764) established the popular title for his new scientific theory, "Common Sense." This is how he defined it in 1764: "Sense means judgment and common sense means common judgment. God has endowed mankind with reason and common sense. By these we judge things that are self-evident and draw conclusions that are not self-evident."

Reid's philosophy was equivalent to the work of the British writer, Francis Bacon (1561–1626), whom he appreciated and who had led the way at the beginnings of modern science. Bacon opposed the dominant philosophical views of Aristotle in his time for reasons very similar to those that led Reid to oppose Hume. Bacon saw Aristotle's ideas as abstruse and unrelated to reality so he campaigned for a new and better form of scientific thinking. He urged people to research as fully and as widely as possible the two books of God, the Bible and nature, and to ensure that their findings from the two books be not unwisely combined. Fundamentalists would do well to remember Bacon's advice and avoid using Bible content as a source of scientific knowledge. This is how Reid, in his book, referred to Bacon's work:

> The rules of inductive reasoning or of a just interpretation of nature have been, with wonderful sagacity, delineated by the genius of Lord Bacon. His *Novum Organum* may justly be called a grammar of the language of nature. It adds greatly to the merit of his work that, at the time it was written, the world had not seen any tolerable model of inductive reasoning from which the rules of it might be copied.

Reid went on to state that the best models of inductive reasoning, which were subsequently developed by Isaac Newton (1642–1727) in his *Principia*, were drawn from Bacon's rules.

In the same year that he published his major work Reid was appointed to the chair of Moral Philosophy at the University of Glasgow. His new school of philosophy had, by this time, been well received throughout Scotland and in many parts of Europe. It was a philosophy that fitted well into Scottish ways of life. There is no tradition of royalty or class distinction in Scotland like those in other European countries. Until very recently private schools were rare and boarding schools even fewer. Universities too were generally non-residential. Reid seemed to have touched a national chord with his system of knowledge that elevated the individual to the status of an expert. Probably for this very reason, in later years common sense science came to be known as the Scottish Philosophy rather than Reid's. The Scottish enlightenment was strongly influenced by Reid's philosophy and the country's evangelical community was equally happy with it. Thus, throughout the 1760s, a bond was established between Scottish universities and evangelical Christians so that when John Witherspoon left Scotland for America in 1768 to take up the presidency of Princeton he brought with him this unified view of enlightenment thought and evangelical Christianity.

Witherspoon had been an outstanding defender of the Scottish evangelical community in the mid–1770s when clashes between fundamentalists and modernists were frequent. They persisted for almost a century until, in the event known locally as the Disruption of 1843, the Church of Scotland split apart and the evangelical community united around the new Free Church of Scotland. Dr. John Macleod, Principal of the Free Church College, Edinburgh, and a well-known theologian, in his book, *Scottish Theology*, looked back on the nature of the extraordinary evangelical link with America. His book came out 70 years after Witherspoon's departure for America and Princeton University. This was how he spoke about him: "John Witherspoon was the leader of the younger evangelical writers, preachers, and churchmen. It was because of his high standing in these areas that he was invited to become president of the College of New Jersey, later known as Princeton University." This pre-independence link between evangelical Scotland and America was destined to affect the course of Christian thinking for the following century and more. Not least among Witherspoon's contribution was his devotion to common sense science.

Impact of Common Sense Science on America

Reid's science might be called a science of freedom because it gave status to ordinary people, enabling each one to be as assured of good judgment as the philosopher. It is no surprise that it became popular in America. Thomas Jefferson knew about Reid's writings and had his book on a recommended book list. He also put it at the center of the curriculum in his new university of Virginia. Undoubtedly Jefferson's famous phrase "self-evident truths" came directly from Reid as did the convictions associated with these truths: "All men are created equal and are endowed by their creator with certain inalienable rights such as life, liberty, and the pursuit of happiness." Witherspoon's work of shaping the curriculum of Princeton University, being involved in the deliberations that led to independence, and perhaps most significant of all, in shaping the thinking of the many leaders who graduated from Princeton must all be accorded significant factors in shaping the new nation. During Witherspoon's time at Princeton, James Madison, the future president, was one of his students, as was also Aaron Burr, a future vice president. In addition, he saw graduate six members of the Continental Congress, nine cabinet officers, twenty-one senators, thirty-nine congressmen, three Supreme Court justices, and numerous others who later served the nation in significant positions. The timing for Witherspoon's work at Princeton was fortuitous. American universities were expanding rapidly in the last quarter of the eighteenth century, increasing five-fold in that time compared with a doubling of the total population.

By introducing the most liberal and most modern improvements of Europe, and bringing along in his luggage several hundred books, Witherspoon was able to give Princeton an accelerated start. He also introduced a concept of Biblical truth that proved to be a valuable resource for fundamentalists. The evangelical Presbyterian community in Scotland from which he came saw Biblical truth as precisely stated propositions. It was matched by a catechism, a set of questions and answers that every Scottish school student had to learn. By so doing, truth became a stable commodity, not subject to historical variables, conveying one message in all times and places. This view was compatible with common sense science and it later provided stability for fundamentalists who saw in the union of evangelicals and national leaders in 1776 the ideal that they wanted to recover. Many years after the time of Witherspoon, after Princeton had established its own Presbyterian Seminary, it was Scottish realism in both science and theology that was taught. The Reformation claim that the Bible was sufficient by itself for every man and woman to understand its meaning fitted well into this Scottish tradition. Its infallible rule of interpretation was this: when there is a question about the true and full sense of any scripture it may be searched and known by other places in Scripture that speak more clearly. Not surprisingly, propositional truths as Biblical verities reappeared again from time to time in twentieth century evangelical America.

On June 22, 1776, Witherspoon was elected to the Continental congress. He took his seat a few days before the fourth of July, and actively participated in the deliberations on the question of a declaration of independence. Witherspoon cast his affirmative vote for independence on July 2, 1776. Five months after signing the Declaration, the British burned his library. Witherspoon served in Congress for six years and was ambitiously involved in his work on more than 100 committees. At the close of the year 1779 he voluntarily retired from congress. By 1870 common sense philosophy had been influential throughout America for a century and had come into use in educational institutions at all levels of learning. God's truth was seen as a single unified system and common sense science equipped every person to understand its moral structure. This science that had inaugurated modern science 200 years earlier was ideally suited to the needs of the new America as already indicated. It was the cement that bound evangelical Christians and the fathers of confederation together in a partnership that seemed indestructible. It also remained as the science of choice among fundamentals.

It would be hard to overstate the challenges that faced America in the last third of the eighteenth century. Even modern-day crises such as the 2001 terrorist destruction of the Twin Towers in New York City or the 2005 devastation of the Gulf coast by Hurricane Katrina seem small by comparison. America in the late 1770s was faced with a loose union of sovereign states, most of them mired in poverty. Ninety percent of the country was agricultural but the land had to be worked with little access to the kind of machinery that would reduce the hardships of the manual work involved. Farmers took short enlistments in the army to supplement their income but the drop in value of America's paper money reduced the value of that one opportunity for improving their lot and, while away in army service, work at home had to be carried on as best they could by wives and children. Everywhere there were tensions as the new, largely unknown form of republicanism began to find its feet and establish some kind of order both in America and internationally. It was into this arena of need that evangelical Christians came to the rescue of the new republic. Shaped by the influence of revivals, churches and groups of evangelicals were populist, democratic, and they identified with the common people, quite unlike those in the traditions of Europe from which they had sprung. It was easy for them to see Christian values in the American Revolution, stamped as it was by Jeffersonian ideals of inalienable rights given to every person by the Creator, rights to life, liberty and the pursuit of happiness.

To the new fledgling government, support from the mass of Christians was just the authentication it needed. Its appreciation resounded again and again in declarations enshrined in constitutional documents that acknowledged dependence on and submission to the God of Creation. Puritans who came to America in search of Christian freedom saw in the new republic the hope of a true heaven on earth, an improvement on Calvin's Geneva. High ideals like these appeared from time to time in the euphoria of dreams for a true Christian nation. Their hopes were strengthened by the impacts of the Scottish Science of Common Sense, a method of thinking that dates back to the Reformation and the earliest forms of modern science, the mode of thinking that Calvin employed in his government of Geneva. Its essence was that every human has an innate ability to see and interpret what he sees, whether it is nature or the Bible. Its immediate source was the writings of Thomas Reid of Aberdeen University whose book Inquiry *into the Human Mind on the Principles of Common Sense*, published in 1764, became a favorite on Thomas Jefferson's bookshelf and influenced his thinking. The words of Reid's best interpreter, Dugald Stewart of Edinburgh University, were welcome in America. Stewart loved revolutions and said at one time that how a government came into being matters less than how it behaves when in office.

The science of common sense gave new status to democracy. It also gave integrity to simple inductive Bible studies, the only kind possible in rural America at that time. Inductive Bible study in its varied forms remained as the norm for biblical studies in evangelical Christianity right up to the present time. When Alexis de Tocqueville came to America in 1835, he noted that in no country of the world is religion so widespread as in America. He added that the religion he observed, unlike Europe, is intimately linked with democracy and freedom and is completely in harmony with the ideals that govern the nation.

The history and evolution of the science of common sense and its relation to inductive Bible study was and is the science that fundamentalists want to impose on both America and biblical interpretation. They want to go back to the Christian America of the 1770s and they are actively at work in the hope of attaining their goal. They see society as having lost its way and they want to restore it to its former Christian foundations. They oppose the theory of evolution because it does not fit the biblical and social thinking of 200 years ago. It might come as a surprise to them that Charles Darwin also used the common sense method of science, the only kind available to him at that time, to think through the implications of his own research and help usher in the multi-faceted kind of science we know now.

Here is what Darwin wrote in 1837 as noted by Daniel Boorstin in *The Discoverers*, in 1985: "I worked on true Baconian principles and without any theory, collecting facts on a wholesale scale, more especially with respect to domesticated productions, by printed inquiries, by conversations with skilled breeders and gardeners, and by extensive reading." It took him a lot more searching and a lot more testing of different hypotheses before he finally published his theory of evolution 22 years later. The unity of state and Christian values throughout America remained strong right up to the time of the Civil War. In the midst of that awful conflict, correspondence from soldiers, both from North and South, to family members back home told of a common loyalty to God and country. Scouts on either side of a stream in a battlefield zone representing opposing sides of the war, would talk freely to one another. Each side would take time for evening prayers. There was a bond that transcended the horror of war's carnage. That bond began to come apart in the years that followed the Civil War, not suddenly but increasingly as the implications of Darwin's Theory of Evolution created problems for those who never had to cope with challenges to their age-old Biblical interpretations.

Princeton maintained a loyalty to its Scottish heritage all through the 19th century, seeing basic truths as unaffected by time and place and affirming that an ordinary person can rightly understand Scripture without the aid of oral tradition or ecclesiastical authority. Princeton's experts saw themselves as impartial scientific observers, gathering information from the Bible and classifying it in terms of propositional truths. Charles Hodge summarized the Princeton view in words like the following: natural science collects and arranges the facts of the external world. Theologians collect the facts of the Bible and systemize them as truths. Hodge went on to say that these truths implied a form of inspiration in which the Holy Spirit inspired the authors of Scripture to select correct words. In 1881 Archibald Alexander Hodge and B. B. Warfield, both of Princeton published their famous defense of Scripture's inerrancy as originally written. It included the statement that the Scriptures not only contain God's word but they are the word of God. Infallible thought must be definite thought, they affirmed, and definite thought is expressed in words. Thus truth in the words of Scripture became an externally stable entity. A Princeton theologian went further to assert that the distinctiveness of Christianity is that it came into the world reasoning its way to dominion. While acknowledging the place of he Holy Spirit, he pointed out that reason must be active if a prepared heart is to respond to God. Unfortunately reason became very inactive for too many fundamentalists.

The Anti-intellectual Underpinnings

The 18th and 19th centuries in America were times of revivals involving mass meetings and large numbers of conversions. No other nation experienced anything comparable. From the 1730s in New England to the Moody campaigns in different places 150 years later these movements, led by gifted evangelicals, were powerful influences within American culture. The revivals that were led by Jonathan Edwards and George Whitefield in the 1830s and 1840s, sometimes described as the great awakening because of their influence across all social lines, focused on "new birth," largely an unknown aspect of evangelical life in 1740. George Whitefield's description of it was as follows: "The doctrine of the new birth made its way like lightning into the hearers' consciences." The churches of New England were augmented by as many as 50,000 converts within a short period of time. All segments of society were affected. Common people responded in huge numbers and so did the social and intellectual elite. Historians have concluded that this revival led directly to the formation of such new universities as Dartmouth and Brown. They also assert that the revolution that followed within a generation would have led to a very different outcome if the revival had not happened. The social world of the New England states had been greatly strengthened by all that had happened. People were ready for a challenge.

Jonathan Edwards' sharp focus on new birth was matched by similar challenges to transformations in individual lives in other revivals. A closer look at these movements reveals an unhealthy attitude to intellectual activity, not because any such thinking was advocated by revivalists but rather because of an unintended consequence of their activities. If one examines the life of D. L. Moody (1837–1899), who was regarded as the greatest evangelist of his century, some of these unintended consequences can be seen. Moody was born on a farm in Northfield, Mass, and as a member of a large family with limited financial resources he left home at he age of 17 to find work in the city. In his late teen years he committed his life to Christ and soon thereafter was launched into his life work, beginning with several urban missions and then going to Britain in 1873 for major campaigns. He returned as a celebrity because of the enormous success of his British missions. It was in Britain that he developed his technique for drawing large crowds by uniting Protestants across denominational lines through saturation publicity in both the secular and religious newspapers. The stir created by this skillful strategy attracted unbelievers who might otherwise never have attended a local church service. Whenever questions arose about theological differences between churches or individuals, Moody always refused to get involved. His characteristic approach in such situations was to urge his friends and associates to leave unrelated questions aside and concentrate on the most important thing, the necessity of every person making a decision to turn to Christ.

While Moody had no intention of suggesting that theological questions were unimportant, the fact that he pushed them aside left the impression that things of the mind were inferior to those of the will. Because he was so influential throughout America, any position he took carried great weight throughout the evangelical community. He rose to fame at a time when individualism was strong and the American dream was seen as a real possibility for every one. Moody's emphasis on the individual and individual sins fitted into this outlook. There were other features of his personality and behavior that added to his popularity. He dressed well, with the air of a businessman going to work, quite unlike other revivalists. His meetings were conducted with relative decorum and the content of his messages was mainly sentiment rather than sensationalism. He emphasized the love of God in all his messages and this approach endeared him to a wide range of protestant groups with whom he might otherwise have major disagreements. Moody used the mass media more than anyone and mass media both then and now were and are overwhelming influences in America, to a far greater extent than in Europe. There it is usually read with some suspicion. If one compares the role of the newspaper in Moody's time with television today, one sees the same technique of a strong leader supported by a powerful medium dominating the world of evangelical fundamentalism.

Moody was loyal to holiness movements and he believed in the premillennial outlook that was associated with the work of J. N. Darby. Both of these movements stressed individual responsibility by living in a close relationship with God at all times and, in so doing, avoiding involvement in what was seen as the surrounding godless world of evil. There was little for the mind either in Moody's campaigns or in the conferences he organized at Northfield, his home community. The emphasis at his conferences was often referred to as letting go to the Holy Spirit and the consistent message at the large campaign sites was the need for decisive acts of the will. It was a similar story with other revivalists. The emphases on biblical inerrancy and infallibility were not things that Moody and others spoke about but it represented how they understood the Bible. The emphasis on specific prophetical interpretations, however, such as the expectation of a silent return of Christ to take away his people, was hardly the kind of situation that would encourage thinking because of the fixed nature of biblical prophecy. Anyone with such an outlook must hold an uncritical understanding of the Bible, one that would preclude any reassessment of its history or authorship.

Some would say that Moody's work and influence continued through the second half of the twentieth century through the life of Billy Graham as his successor. The similarities between the two men are quite striking. Both maintained a simple message, a call to repent and a demand that every one who did repent must also surrender to the authority of Jesus Christ. The source of their claim to be speaking for God was always based on verses from the Bible. The second overall similarity was the ability of each to unite and gain for their campaigns the support of all segments of Protestant Christendom. Whether the similarity between Moody and Billy Graham is true, it is certainly true that Moody's influence and methods, mainly through his close friend R. A. Torrey, became a dominant force in the formation of *The Fundamentals*. Just as Moody was able to gain support from a broad range of Protestantism so the authors of the books that were written between 1910 and 1915 were able to secure broad support from the whole evangelical community. That, of course, collapsed after the Scopes Trial, and evangelicalism has been a divided community ever since.

Learning the Bible by Induction

Common sense science did not vanish as modern forms took over. Its inductive model became the almost universal standard for Bible study by evangelicals both then and now. It would be difficult to find, today, a single small group Bible study either within churches or in homes that did not use the same old inductive method as *The Fundamentalists* employed. Even in places where evangelicals are fully aware of the errors in the Biblical text, induction is still the norm in the study of the Bible. Take for example the following series of study questions on Genesis chapters one and two, taken from a widely-used publication titled *Inductive Studies of the Bible for Students and Church Groups*, then consider the implications of this kind of study with the words of Bruce Waltke, already quoted in this chapter in the section dealing with the evolution of the higher criticism: (1) What made Adam and Eve different from the rest of creation? (2) What responsibilities and privileges did God give that first man and woman? (3) How did God evaluate his special creation? (4) What restrictions on human activity did God set? (5) When God brought Adam and Eve together, what principles did he establish for married life? Bruce Waltke says that Genesis chapters one and two are myths. He explains his use of this word by saying that they are stories that relate to the activities of God among humans.

He also adds that the words "history" and "science," as we understand them today, carry no meaning for these first two chapters of Genesis. He says that we need to know the customs of the times that relate to these chapters if we are going to understand what is written about them. If we now add to these observations the truth of the theory of evolution we encounter additional difficulties when we try to compare the findings of modern biology concerning humans with the narrative of Genesis. One well-known evangelical theologian from Cambridge, England, who happens to be conversant with and supportive of the theory of evolution, has written about Genesis chapters one and two but in a very different style to that of the inductive study authors. His name is Derek Kidner and this is how he introduces the part of Genesis dealing with the origin of human life:

> There are two quite different accounts given to Christians today, one a short account from Genesis, describing a creature fashioned from earthly matter yet God-like, the other a mosaic of many fragments from paleontology depicting a species fashioned over perhaps a million years or more into the present human form, showing the characteristics of modern humans as far back as 20,000 years ago.

The question that arises is this: does inductive Bible study provide an accurate or an inaccurate understanding of the meaning of Genesis? An examination of the twentieth century's practice of induction may help answer this question.

No one has pioneered the teaching of inductive Bible study as strongly or as consistently as Robert A. Traina. As a man loyal to traditional views of the Bible he felt that a gap had developed between what evangelicals believed and what the Bible said. He developed in some detail the inductive method and its practical application, combining its insights with the tools of traditional exegesis and setting out the results in his book, *Methodical Bible Study*, in 1952. It became a popular book, was translated into several languages, used in scores of colleges and seminaries around the world, and subsequently recognized as the standard text on the inductive method of Bible study. This was how he summarized his method in the 1952 publication:

"There are two main approaches to Bible study. One is deductive. It begins with generalizations and moves for their support to the particulars. By its very nature deduction tends to be subjective and prejudicial. It produces those who dictate to scripture rather than listen to it. Induction is objective and impartial. It demands that one first examine the particulars of scripture so that one's conclusions are based on those particulars. Such an approach is sound because, being objective, it corresponds to the objective nature of scripture. It produces hearers rather than speakers."

There is a strong similarity to common sense science in this description of inductive Bible study as one would expect. Scripture is treated as something completely removed from personal experience or bias, an objective reality that can be examined just as one would examine the physical environment around us. By collecting data from various verses, one arrives at the meaning of the Bible just as one would have done by the older scientific methods and just as many of the authors who wrote for *The Fundamentals* did. If one now considers modern historical methods instead of modern biological science, one finds that historians never base their conclusions on specific bits of documents that they collect. Instead, they look for underlying patterns among their sources of information and once these patterns are identified they become keys to open the meanings in subsequent findings of documents. To restate this way of thinking as it might apply to Genesis, one looks for trends, repetitive ways of saying similar things, and implied purposes that may be seen as governing all of these, in order to come up with a meaning that lies beneath the actual words rather than in them. This kind of thinking would never occur to most fundamentalists. For such, every word of the Bible carries a value equal to any biblical word. Thus, biblical reading for comprehension becomes a task like building a house;

one collects suitable bricks and puts them together to create a beautiful edifice.

R. A. Torrey, one of D. L. Moody's closest friends and the senior leader in the creation of *The Fundamentals*, expressed, in 1900, the nature of this inductive method in the following way: "The Bible teaches us to use a rigidly inductive method, one that uses the methods of modern science applied to the Bible. It includes a thorough analysis followed by careful synthesis. The result is a careful, unbiased, systematic, thorough-going, inductive study and statement of biblical truth." By modern science Torrey meant common sense or Baconian science. His view of the Bible, just like Traina's, saw it as an authority to guide people in ways that are completely removed from their experiences, biases, and purposes, like a referee in a game that they might be playing. This view of scripture as an objective reality totally independent of human involvement both in its creation and utilization is one that was popular in the thirteenth century. Fifty years after the publication of his *Methodical Bible Study*, Traina was honored by a national religious organization as the world's foremost thinker on inductive Bible study. On the occasion of this event he reflected on his thinking about induction. The overwhelming conviction that had developed in his mind over the years was the growing chasm between (a) belief that scripture and the God of scripture are the supreme authority for faith and practice and (b) actions, as it is what one does that defines what they believe.

Traina lists the causes as he sees them that gave rise to the growing chasm between belief and action. His first was the failure to test both faith and action against specific biblical texts. He includes in his use of the phrase specific biblical texts the analysis of their grammatical, historical, and literary contexts but rejects all kinds of perspectives that come from outside of scripture itself. Just as he had outlined in his book 50 years earlier, so now he sees the Bible as an objective reality completely independent of human experience. His second cause of the chasm was the failure to develop biblical theology from specific biblical texts, particularly any or all of the texts from both old and new testaments. In support of this view he refers to Brevard Child who wrote, "Both testaments of the Bible are witnesses to a common objective subject matter who is Jesus Christ." Traina's third cause brings him back to his first love, the proper use of inductive study leading to inferential reasoning. This is the view of the Bible that persists at the present time in Bible study. It is the view that is high-lighted in the quotation at the head of this chapter and it was and is the view of fundamentalists who stick to the old common sense science. It is a view that cannot be sustained in the light of modern scholarship. It is a view that is contradicted again and again within the Bible itself as, first, the Old Testament prophets went beyond the actual words of the Bible to find their meaning, and second, when Jesus went beyond the written record to explain the meaning of the words that were said to have been inscribed on stone by the hand of God.

4

Circling the Wagons,
1910 to 1915

*Man was created, not evolved. He did not come by descent from
fish or ape but at once, direct, full made, from God.*
                                    —The Rev Dyson Hague,
                                    Vol. 8, *The Fundamentals*

The title of this chapter is taken from South African history. In that country, prior to the Second Anglo-Boer War of 1899, the Afrikaner population migrated northward into new territory where they frequently encountered large, well-armed Zulu tribes. To defend themselves they would arrange their wagons in a circle and take up positions inside the circle. They could thus avoid many of the Zulu arrows and spears and, at the same time, counterattack with superior weapons. It was the only kind of action they could take in such a hostile environment and it proved to be successful. At the beginning of the twentieth century, fundamentalists found themselves in a situation very much like the South African one. They felt surrounded by a hostile environment of modernism and there was a cry for something to be done to defend against it. The Bible was under attack by the authors of the higher criticism, and evolution was seen as a godless attack on the foundations of the Christian life. Dyson Hague's quote from *The Fundamentals* is a good indication of the mood of the times. All that was needed was a leader to organize the fundamentalist wagons and mount a defense. Lyman and Milton Stewart proved to be the leadership that emerged to do this work.

Higher criticism was examined in the previous chapter, the first of the modernist developments that was strongly opposed by fundamentalists. The issue there was quite clear: the critics had changed the infallible Bible and upset all the interpretations that had been built on the existing translation. The higher critics were applying modern techniques in historical analysis but this aspect of their work was largely ignored. What mattered was just one thing: the fundamentalists no longer had one inerrant translation and this to them was unacceptable. In the second issue of modernism that was rejected, that of Darwin's theory of evolution, a very different problem is encountered. Here it is clear to all that a different kind of science is involved. The older, common sense or Baconian science, was familiar and was regularly used by fundamentalists but evolutionary science was employing fundamentally different methods. What it was introducing was a completely new paradigm for scientific study and, as Thomas Kuhn, the historian of science, had pointed out, science advances by a series of revolutions, not by gradual change. The paradigm shift from common sense science to Darwin's theory of evolution was far greater than anyone had experienced in three centuries. It was too big for fundamentalists and they rejected it outright.

Chapter 3 showed how the Scottish philosophy of common sense fit so well into evangelical thinking that independence from Britain and the emergence of the new nation came together in a powerful unity of thought, faith and purpose. John Witherspoon's role in this phase of American life was crucial to the success of this union. The very nature of the Scottish Presbyterian theology coupled with common sense science, had an enduring quality that persisted into the eighteenth century and remained strong right up to the time of the American Civil War. In other words it had been the traditional norm for more than 150 years in American life for evangelicals and government leaders alike when Darwin's new science burst upon the Christian community. This collision with modernism came earlier in Europe. In America it arrived more slowly. There were arguments and clashes of opinions regarding Darwin for some time after 1859 before the theory became universally accepted. At Princeton, as well as in much of the rest of nineteenth century Protestant America, the concept that an ordinary person could rightly understand Scripture was firmly entrenched. Even as late as 1925, A. C. Dixon, who had been the principal organizer of *The Fundamentals*, defended the old science in these words: "I believe in the scientific method of gaining and verifying knowledge by exact observation and correct thinking."

To complicate matters, as explained in the last chapter, common sense science, inductive approaches to acquisition of knowledge, did not remain time sensitive. It was not tied to a particular period of time. It became and still is today the way evangelicals study their Bibles. While its use as a scientific methodology is dated, it remains very much alive in numerous Christian communities. The new science represented by the theory of evolution was such a big leap from the old that, for many, the transfer of allegiance could only be envisaged as being acceptable by a new generation, one that would be acclimatized to new ways of thinking. It is difficult for fundamentalists to make this transition today because so much of their apologetic and prophetic interpretations of Scripture are based on common sense science. The newer models of science see perception as an interpretive process. Speculative theories are acceptable, not as theories in the dictionary sense, but as valid inferences from the facts. No serious modern scientist doubts the validity of this approach. As this book comes to the study of *The Fundamentals*, the unwavering rejection of any changes to biblical content and the opposition to the theory of evolution soon become clear. The quotation at the head of Chapter 2 holds true.

The Fundamentals

The venture that was to define fundamentalism for the rest of the century and beyond began in the mind of Lyman Stewart (1840–1923), a wealthy Californian business man who—with his brother Milton—had achieved success in the oil business, becoming chief stockholders of the Union Oil Company. While Milton was supportive of the publishing venture that was about to begin, the inspiration and interest lay with Lyman who had been contributing to different Christian enterprises for some time and had difficulty making up his mind whether he should stay in business or devote all of his time and energy to the support of Christian organizations. In previous years he had given financial support to the Bible Institute of Los Angeles, Occidental College of Los Angeles, and various publishing projects. His brother Milton focused his efforts on overseas Christian missions. Lyman Stewart's uncertainty over how he should direct his energies seemed to become clear to him in a letter to his brother as *The Fundamentals* were being published. He told his brother that he saw the support of Christian work a great deal better use of his time that dealing with business matters. The two brothers were born in Pennsylvania where they speculated in oil but with little success. It was some time later, after they moved to Los Angeles that their investments in oil led to a better outcome.

Stewart had a passion to counter what he saw as widespread unbelief coupled with attacks on the integrity of the Bible by higher criticism. The latter of these two, the one that was examined in Chapter 3, had a particular grip on his mind because he subscribed to the concept of premillennialism. This aspect of Christendom, launched by Darby in earlier years and promoted by Scofield in the 1909 edition of his Bible, emphasized the possibility of an unexpected return of Jesus, invisible to all not involved and carrying serious consequences for all Christians. This teaching necessarily gave a great sense of urgency to Christian work and, in Stewart's mind, a challenge to do everything possible to stem what he perceived as a tide of anti–Christian evils. He had already supported publications that reinforced traditional values and beliefs and he felt that the series of books now being designed would serve the same purpose. The prophecies that told of the invisible return of Jesus were tied to the infallible and inerrant Bible that Stewart and those who thought like him were using and which was now under attack. The second threat came from Darwin's book of 1859, *The Origin of Species*. This challenge to the Christian community was not immediately as influential as the higher criticism because very few understood what it was all about or how it affected Christian belief. Furthermore, for some time after its publication it was mired in controversy and opposing theories. As this chapter will show, its full force, when it finally hit, influenced all of America.

The 12 volumes of *The Fundamentals* appeared between 1910 and 1915. The details of each volume and the background information that accompanied them are all listed in Appendix A. As will readily be seen, it was a massive publishing venture, even by present-day standards. To have arranged authors for the 90 chapters in the 12 volumes to whom little or no payment was made, organize a non-incorporated publishing house in Chicago, arrange an editorial board, mail out to a selected list of preachers, theologians, editors of religious journals, missionaries and others approximately three million copies of each book, all represented a magnificent feat. These volumes were sent out all over the English-speaking world. To maintain anonymity in it all Stewart made sure that the cover of each book was titled as follows, *The Fundamentals: A Testimony to the Truth, Compliments of Two Christian Laymen.* The authors came from the United States for the most part. About eight of them came from Canada, the same number from Scotland, and the same number from England. A few other countries contributed one each. At first glance most of the chapters seem to be restatements of basic historic Christian teachings: the divinity, virgin birth, incarnation and resurrection of Jesus, the person of The Holy Spirit, and some statements about Biblical interpretations. A closer look at the contents of chapters reveals the heart of each one, an attack on those who have tried to interfere with its ancient infallibility and inerrancy. When chapters on evolution are examined it will be seen that they are vitriolic rather than critical. Most of the comments consist of outright ridicule of Darwin's theory of evolution.

Stewart asked Amzi Clarence Dixon, then pastor of Moody Church in Chicago and in his mid-fifties, to coordinate the publishing project. He was aided by Louis Meyer and Reuben Torrey. Stewart described the author team that emerged as the best and most loyal Bible teachers in the world and added that their writings will be masterpieces. Both the writers and the organizers of *The Fundamentals* represented all of the different kinds of Christian loyalties that were found in evangelical America: Revivalists, Holiness emphasis, Premillennials and Postmillennials, Pentecostalists, and those who representing the different church denominations. While each one remained loyal to the particular beliefs held and in most cases were active in promoting them, they put these differences aside during the writing of the 12 books in order to present a unified fundamentalist position. They were anxious to show thereby that they were united on the fundamentals of evangelical beliefs in spite of the different emphases they held as individuals. They wanted to secure support from all evangelicals by so doing. For various reasons the opposite effect occurred. The publications were not well received by the media, neither the secular nor the religious, and by the time of the Scopes Trial in 1925 the separation of fundamentalists from other evangelicals was evident to all.

Evolution Is Rejected

Several authors of *The Fundamentals* attacked the theory of evolution, some from a background of science, others from little of no knowledge of either scientific methodology or Darwin's work. Later in this chapter, as the peak of anti-evolutionary activity in the Scopes Trial is examined, the work of William Jennings Bryan (1860–1925) will get a close look. The drawing of him at the end of this chapter was based on photos taken in 1925, the year in which he died. Like George Frederick Wright (1838–1921) and a number of other authors of *The Fundamentals*, Bryan was already an older man when he became involved in the 1925 trial of John Scopes. As a result, the pictures from Bryan's campaigns against evolution as well as from the writings of the years 1910 to 1915 represent a long term evangelical perspective on evolution, one that extends back into the last quarter of the nineteenth century. Wright wrote the first chapter of Volume Seven. It was titled "The Passing of Evolution" and it dealt in some detail with the numerous counter arguments that had been advanced in the wake of the publication of Darwin's *Origin of Species* in 1859. Wright was by far the most competent of the authors who critically attacked evolution so his presentation will be examined more closely than those of the others.

Wright's background comes from the older and intellectually sophisticated New England Calvinism. He was well known as both a theologian and an earth scientist. He had been editor of a most respected theological journal so it was appropriate that he write the two other chapters that carry his name and deal with controversial aspects of Biblical interpretation. He defended Asa Gray's view of Darwinism when it was unpopular to do so and, as a result, many of his more conservative evangelicals criticized him. Asa Gray was the first person with whom Charles Darwin shared his theory of evolution. That occurred several years before the theory was published. Wright defended Gray's theistic view of evolution, namely that it was designed and directed by God. Darwin disagreed with this view of the methodology employed but the two scholars remained good friends. It was Darwin's choice of natural selection as the mechanism for evolution that caused most of the problems about getting his theory accepted. Nowadays no one suggests that natural selection is the only mechanism involved, but in Wright's day it was widely accepted as the one and only simply because Darwin had proposed it. Wright was still regarded as a conservative evangelical in 1910. They knew his views on evolution. His involvement in *The Fundamentals* was further evidence of the organizers' desire to make common ground, if they could, with all evangelicals.

Wright's opening statement is a good indication of the widespread acceptance of natural selection as the one and only mechanism of evolution: "the widely current doctrine of evolution which we are now compelled to combat is one which practically eliminates God from the whole creative process." He goes on at length to discuss the nature of species, the extraordinary range of different animals alive at the present time, and the impossibility of all of them developing from one ancestor. Along the way he injects the observation that Darwin did not assume a natural cause for the origin of life but rather accepted it as due to the action of God. It is easy to see how a person, even one as knowledgeable as Wright, who did not have Darwin's extensive exposure to biological research, would hesitate to accept the common origin of all life forms. The time being considered was still half a century away from the discovery of DNA, the one event that so clearly demonstrated the ubiquity of common genes. The second problem that Wright had to face, again without the knowledge of today, was the age of the earth. Anyone could see that, if small changes were to add up to the enormous varieties of life forms seen today, an enormous amount of time would be needed. The approximately four billions of years known now for the age of the earth were unknown in Wright's day. One of Darwin's earlier estimates was a third of a billion years but, though inadequate, it was uniformly rejected by all scientists. Lord Kelvin, Britain's foremost physicist in post–Darwinian times, was convinced that the earth could not be older than 30 million years.

Wright's clearest and greatest difficulty with Darwin relates to the emergence of humans. In his mind, "The failure of evolution to account for humans is conspicuous." He lists a set of uniquely human attributes and goes over the details of each one, concluding that their nature and variety would require the simultaneous development of each one of these attributes. Having made this assertion he concludes, "such chance combinations are beyond all possibility of rational belief." Unfortunately for Wright, a similar unique analysis could be made for any other species of mammals but it would provide no more help for understanding how it evolved than would the list for humans. As one reads further in this chapter on "The Passing of Evolution" it becomes clear that Wright is comfortable with many aspects of Darwin's theory until some aspect of it collides with a particular biblical interpretation. At that point in the narrative, the writer jumps to biblical information to explain the evolution of humans: "animals differ from humans in so many particulars that it is necessary to suppose that humans came into existence as the Bible represents, by the special creation of a single pair, from whom all the varieties of the race have sprung." This is precisely the kind of thinking that prevents rational thought. It is a denial of the basic rule that even in medieval times was respected, that the two "books" of God, Bible and nature, must be studied independently.

The remainder of Wright's paper provides additional evidence of the wrong use of biblical information. At one point he concludes that it is impossible to get any proof of evolution that would modify the conception of Christianity. Finally, in his concluding paragraph, he berates those who consider the results of scientific research as relevant to religious matters because they have no value there. Here, as in the earlier example, the writer is assessing scientific data in terms of their relation to biblical truth instead of retaining them as separate, different, but equal sources of truth. James Orr from Scotland was a well-known scholar and, like Wright, one that was not afraid to stand away from fundamentalist dogma when it was indefensible. Although he did not say so in any of his four chapters for the *Fundamentals*, in order to maintain unity, he did not accept the claim that the Bible is infallible and inerrant. Two of Orr's chapters deal with the theory of evolution in some detail; the first, "Science and Christian Faith," is firstly an excellent discussion about keeping the study of the Bible and nature separate yet holding each part of equal value in its own domain, and secondly it is a model analysis for its time of Darwin's theory of evolution. One wishes the others who wrote about evolution at the same time had made some effort to study this chapter of Barr's. One also wishes that today's misguided critics of evolution would read it before claiming to be the rightful successors to *The Fundamentals*. Orr's other chapter, "The Early Narratives of Genesis" is weak. It makes some strong factual claims of historicity where none exist.

In his chapter on "Science and Christian Faith," Orr asks, "What does the Bible claim for itself in relation to science?" He then answers his own question both negatively and positively, pointing out first that people say there are clashes between the Bible and science where none exist. His positive answer is that the biblical design is to reveal God and his will, not to explain nature. Thus natural things are referred to in simple, popular language. He illustrates this point by referring to talking about the sun rising and setting, hardly an accurate scientific statement but in no way a misleading one. What Orr is saying, and this is only summarizing his viewpoint, is that people battle over interpretations of the Bible, not facts, when they discuss science and Christian faith. Scientists tend to affirm that their work contradicts the Bible while Christians may insist that the Bible can be seen as a record of the latest scientist discoveries. As he goes on to discuss Darwin's theory of evolution, Orr maintains the same view as before, that people perceive contradictions where there are none. He continues with what must have been a new perspective on Darwin's work to all the other authors working with him, certainly new to Wright who assumed that natural selection was the only mechanism of evolution that anyone had ever suggested. Orr argued that the evidence for the theory of evolution was strong but the notion that it must have occurred via random natural processes of the kind with which people are familiar was quite unacceptable. By breaking new ground in this way, Orr led the way to what is now known so well, that there are many mechanisms at work as living things change over time.

The recognition of multiple mechanisms was a major achievement for Orr, given the viewpoint of so many of his colleagues and of the desire of the organizers to maintain unity of outlook in their opposition to evolution. However, as he continued to examine evolution in relation to human life, Orr began to slip in his earlier devotion to the separation of investigations into the Bible from those relating to nature. As he listed the self-conscious, self-directed, rational, and moral characteristics of humans and showed thereby that they were quite different from animal consciousness, Orr concluded that humans could not therefore have evolved as a slow development from the animal stage. "The human body," said Orr, "must have come from a special act of the Creator. His origin may have been as sudden as Genesis represents." The big mistake in Orr's reasoning, one that is not supported by biblical statements, is the assumption that the uniqueness of humans means unique bodies. This is not a biblical view. If one chooses to argue from Genesis, the source used by Orr, one can see that there is nothing unique about the dust of the ground, the raw material that God used to create humans. In his chapter on "The Early Narratives of Genesis," Orr is far too defensive of traditional Biblical interpretations. One gets the impression that he has a set of these interpretations guiding him rather than the best findings from modern science. He even goes so far as to say, "Future forms of the theory of evolution will likely be in harmony with the Biblical account." This is just the opposite of the kind of thinking he advocated so eloquently in his chapter on "Science and Christian Faith."

To conclude Orr's observations on Genesis, he appears to be more strongly on the defensive when it comes to Noah's Flood than in other parts of early Genesis. His statements are entirely inappropriate for records that are so old and for events that bear so little relation to existing knowledge. Noah's flood is described as an actual historical occurrence. Orr does not say if he is using the word historical in its present meaning. It seems that this is what he is doing as he follows later in the chapter with this statement: "The flood was an historical fact, and the preservation of Noah and his family is one of the best and most widely attested of human traditions." These statements can usefully be compared with the interpretive accounts of Genesis in Chapter Six, particularly the documentation of the real history as understood today of the so-called Noah's Flood.

Dyson Hague's chapter, "Doctrinal Value of First Chapters of Genesis" (a short quote from which appears at the head of this chapter), gives strong defensive statements about evolution. It is clear that the voice of modern science carries no weight here. That would have been all right if the chapter had been written as a theological paper. It was not. Early on, Hague says, "We assume from the start the historicity of Genesis." That is the kind of statement that a scientist can and does challenge but Hague makes no effort to explain his use of the word historicity when clearly he means by it something quite different, namely his interpretation of the Bible.

From the naïve initial statement that everything he has to say is historically trustworthy, Hague attacks the foundations of Darwin's theory of evolution, not by using evidence that can be verified, but instead by abusive language directed at the content of Darwin's work. Here is one example of his rhetoric: "when you read what writers say about humans and their bestial origins, your shoulders unconsciously droop; your head hangs down; your heart feels sick." As Hague sees things, the Bible, and therefore he, stands plainly against the theory that all species, vegetable and animal, originated through evolution from lower forms of life. It soon becomes clear as one reads on that Hague has little knowledge of how the theory of evolution was developed. He says that species cannot be transformed into new species. In his mind they are immutable. Biological scientists know that this is not true because they have observed it happening again and again. In summary Hague, like so many other fundamentalists, decided that Darwin's theory is bad because it seems to contradict a particular interpretation of the Bible. No amount of extra-biblical evidence can change a mindset of this kind.

The last two chapters of anti-evolutionary talk that will be discussed here from *The Fundamentals* come from Chapter Eight. The first one is titled "Evolution in the Pulpit." It consists for the most part of an extended series of statements, each rejecting all aspects of evolution. The introduction to the chapter begins in the following way: "Darwin's theory of evolution is based on hypothesis only. It was and still is, after the lapse of 40 years, without a single known fact to support it."

The rest of the paper goes on to add additional invective, finally confusing Darwin's theory with the philosophies of Spencer. It is difficult to imagine why this paper was included in a venture that aimed at stating and reinforcing the basic teachings of historic Christianity. The second chapter, titled "Decadence of Darwinism," is equally mindless. Like the first chapter it mocks every claim in the basic theory. The writer's conclusion is that " The statement that Darwinism is an approved science is the most deplorable feature of the whole wretched propaganda." After allowing for the lack of present-day knowledge when these two chapters were written, it remains difficult to understand how responsible individuals could write such a mishmash of unrelated opinions and guesses. It is equally difficult to comprehend the wisdom of the organizers of *The Fundamentals* who selected these writers, accepted their works, and distributed millions of copies of their chapters all over the world in books that were titled, "A Testimony to the Truth." One can only assume that, embedded in the minds of the men who organized the set of publications known as *The Fundamentals*, there was a hatred of opinions that opposed their own. Hatred of contrary views is no way to defend truth. It must be shared with the kind of intellectual humility that was so elegantly demonstrated in Darwin's life. Fortunately some wisdom surfaced at a later date, in 1917, when most of the 90 chapters were republished in a four-volume edition and these two chapters were excluded.

William Jennings Bryan (1860–1925)

As has already been noted, Bryan represents the peak of opposition to Darwin's theory of evolution as it was expressed in the Scopes Trial. That trial might not have impacted America in the way it did if the principals on both sides of the issue as well as others who attended had not been such well-known figures all across America. As it happened, the outcome had huge national repercussions, branding forever the nature of fundamentalism. Bryan's opposition to evolution goes back much further than either *The Fundamentals* or the Scopes Trial. It became a part of his life. He arrived on the American scene about the same time as Darwin's *Origin of Species* and the two were in opposition to each other from the time that Bryan was in college. From that time on his sights were set on a political life. In his valedictory at the end of his college years he said he wanted to be involved in some way with the United States Senate. All across the country Bryan fought evolution. Here is one of his statements: "The evolutionary hypothesis is the only thing that has seriously menaced religion since the birth of Christ, and it menaces all other religions as well." As we consider Bryan's high standing in the life of America from the 1890s on, it is obvious that any legal position he might take against evolution would impact every American.

At the age of 30, William Jennings Bryan, a self-declared fundamentalist, was elected a Democratic congressman for Nebraska, quite a contrast to the situation 100 years later when fundamentalism became almost a synonym for the Republican Party. Six years after his election to Congress, Bryan received the nomination of the Democratic Party for the presidency of the United States. He had achieved the reputation of being a powerful, even eloquent, speaker and his words of acceptance at his nomination in 1896 went down in history as one of the most memorable political speeches ever heard in American campaigns. His theme was "Shall we crucify America on a cross of gold?" by which he meant is it right to tie America to currency standards designed to help the rich business interests of New England against the interest of rural America? It was a reaction from small-town, agricultural America that Bryan felt he represented against the powerful business and political power of the New England states. The applause at the convention went on for more than an hour and its political impact lasted for a long time. Bryan lost the election that followed but he was nominated again in 1900 and yet once more in 1908. He lost on both of these occasions too but his popularity remained. President Woodrow Wilson appointed him to the position of Secretary of State but he resigned in 1917 in protest against America's entry into World War I. War was not the only point of difference between Bryan and Wilson. When asked in 1920 if he believed in Darwin's theory of evolution, Wilson replied: "You mean they are still arguing about the truth of that after all these years?"

Bryan tied his Christian faith tightly to morality, a conviction that was picked up later in the Moral Majority Movement. He did not seem to understand that morality has multiple roots. He was unable to conceive of justice and doing the right thing as values that would be accepted by humanity apart from a system of rewards and punishments. He felt that belief in God and in Christ, together with a belief in life after death, all were indispensable components of morality. In essence, Bryan was saying that humanity could do no good without a responsibility to God and to the Bible. Without the restraint of such a higher authority the naturally wicked impulses of himself and people in general would destroy society. Once he indicated he was terrified at the thought that only one letter separated immortality from immorality. He felt it was the duty of every Christian to combat everything that would weaken dependence on God. From such a position came the virulence of his hatred of evolution in words like these: "I know there is one menace to fundamental morality: it is Darwin's hypothesis that links humanity to lower forms of life, making us all lineal descendants of the brute. All the virtues that rest upon our religious ties to God are thus weakened." In the years following his departure from Wilson's cabinet, Bryan campaigned against evolution across the country, using his political stature to persuade state legislatures to enact laws that would prohibit the teaching of evolution in schools.

He had an interesting view of the rights of teachers, one that would not easily be defended today and it came up when he discovered that 17 states had forbidden the reading of the Bible in schools. He said that something must be done about it and asked the question, "Shall teachers, paid by taxation, be allowed to teach unproven theories of science that undermine the faith of young people?" By unproved, of course, he meant Darwin's theory of evolution. He continued the argument with states and school boards and asserted on one occasion, when speaking to the Legislature of the State of West Virginia, "The one who writes the check rules the school." On that same occasion he urged the legislators to ban the teaching of evolution in all the schools of the state. In his publication *Seven Questions in Dispute* Bryan added more about his understanding of the rights of teachers: "If a teacher of evolution insists that he should be permitted to teach whatever he pleases, regardless of the wishes of the taxpayers, the answer is obvious. He should teach what he is employed to teach, just as a painter uses the colors that his employer desires." Here, as on so many other occasions, Bryan's ignorance of the meaning of the theory of evolution leads him to present spurious arguments: "Why should we allow teachers to deny the existence of God whose name is on our coins, or to scoff at the Bible which our President uses when he takes the oath of office."

In year after year from 1921 to 1924 he lectured on evolution across the country, asking legislatures to ban the teaching of evolution in all their schools. He succeeded in persuading Florida to do this and, in 1925, achieved the same result with Tennessee. That last-named one was destined to be the locale of his final and unsuccessful fight against evolution. At the University of Wisconsin he got into a heated argument about evolution with the university's president. It led to his opponent saying that his lectures were more likely to make atheists than believers. Alongside the cross-country campaigns and lectures Bryan promoted the work of two organizations that shared his views, The Supreme Kingdom and Bible Crusaders. Bryan was better known across America than any other leading politician when the announcement was made, in 1925, of an anti-evolution trial in Tennessee. In the little town of Dayton, where the trial was to take place, as soon as it became known that Bryan was to lead the attack on evolution, people arrived in large numbers to watch the proceedings. Some of the best-known newspaper reporters came too. In the context of Bryan's long-standing campaign against evolution they knew that this event would carry national interest. Radio was just beginning to be used as a means of communication at this time and Dayton was destined to be one of the first places in America to broadcast nationally the proceedings of a trial as it was being conducted.

The Trial of John Scopes

There was another context in addition to Bryan's activities affecting the events that shaped the 1925 trial in Dayton. It was a series of post World War I events that concentrated people's attention on evolution and contributed to the extraordinarily deep imprint of the trial on all of America, an imprint that is still evident today. In Chapter 1, this book pointed out that misunderstandings about Darwin led to social applications of his theory that suggested societies could evolve like animals as they competed for survival. Karl Marx was attracted to this view of evolution and applied it to class struggles in society. Stephen Jay Gould also tended to support it and, since he was the leading American expert on Darwin's work, his ideas received widespread support. Thus, when the Russian Revolution of 1917 occurred, people saw it as one more example of the evils of evolution. It could, as they saw it, destroy morality, reject God, and return humanity to the life of the jungle. The excesses of the Russian revolutionaries in the years after 1917 gave additional support to this view. This revolution represented the first time that the ideas of Karl Marx became the official policy of a major country and both America and Europe were deeply troubled by it.

The human environment in which communism took hold in Russia were equally troubling. The whole Western world of Europe and America was in shock from the horrors of World War I. Five million soldiers had been killed and an additional 20 million injured. The dead and wounded were frequently left where they fell. Starvation was used as a weapon to obtain surrender and poison gas, against all the understandings of international law, was used for the first time in battlefields. Brutality and social disintegration became commonplace and there was a sense that Western Europe, the world's center of culture and science, had descended into deep degradation. The war to end all wars, as the 1914 to 1918 conflict was called, had created more problems than it solved. That was not the whole story. Whether as a result of the horrors of the war or for other reasons, new discoveries of science and new rawness in literature appeared. D. H. Lawrence, the English novelist, typified the avant-garde writers of the time with his advocacy of sexual freedom and the glorification of whatever is natural. About the same time, in the years following the war, Sigmund Freud's books appeared. He had done pioneer work on the human subconscious at the beginning of the century but few took note of his work until the early 1920s. His negative attitudes to religious faith, often treating it as a hangover from the frustration of early childhood, added to the fears of fundamentalists.

In 1919 Albert Einstein's theory of relativity was validated in a sighting of gravitational activity during an eclipse. Ordinarily, a technical development of this kind would only be of interest to specialists but, in the disturbed social environment of 1919, someone decided to call the event the proof of relativism. No longer were there any moral standards. Everything was relative. Young people no longer cared whether their behavior was acceptable to adult norms and the roaring twenties were born. Rampant individualism became popular. To fundamentalists and to adults in general the time had come to put a stop to all this social decay. In most minds it was all the result of Darwinism. Evolution had to be banished from the schools. Fundamentalists launched an attack all across America on all references to evolution in the biological curricula of schools. In state legislatures across the country, in the 1920s, more than 30 bills were proposed, each advocating the abolition of evolution in the content of school curricula. Tennessee was one of the first states to pass a law forbidding the teaching of evolution in all public educational institutions. This was the wording of the act that passed into state law in 1925: "It shall be unlawful for any teacher in any of the universities, normals, and all other public schools of the state which are supported in whole or in part by the public school funds of the state, to teach any theory that denies the story of the divine creation of man as taught in the Bible, and to teach instead that man has descended from a lower order of animals."

Dayton was a small town in the Tennessee Valley between Chattanooga and Knoxville with fewer than 2,000 people in 1925. The overall economy of the town and its surrounding area was not good. Ever since the Coal and Iron Company went bankrupt 10 years earlier, people had been leaving to find work elsewhere. Local civic leaders made efforts to attract new industry but with little success. They opened a high school to improve the educational level of the community and hired a young man, John T. Scopes, who had just completed his training. Robinson's drug store on main street Dayton was the place where people got together in 1925 and dreamed of ways to make their town more than just another farming community. The opportunity to do just that arrived one day as the new teacher and a chemical engineer named George W. Rappleyea were chatting in Robinson's store. Scopes was asked if he taught the content of the biology text provided and he said he did. Rappleyea then pointed out to Scopes that he was in violation of the new law of the state and, after some persuading, convinced the teacher that he should welcome a court challenge on the matter. Rappleyea, who saw in this the opportunity everyone sought, some event that would heighten interest in Dayton, went to the court next day and had a warrant issued for the arrest of Scopes. At the same time Rappleyea sent a telegram to the American Civil Liberties Union in New York. He knew that they were looking for an opportunity to defend the rights of anyone teaching evolutionary theory.

It was the perfect setting for a clash between rural and big city America and the stage was set when Scopes was arrested on May 09, 1925, and a trial arranged for the following day. Tensions between rural and big city America ran high at the time and they constituted much of Bryan's speeches as he traveled across the country defending the rights of the person he called the common man. In response to local appeals Bryan agreed to defend the Tennessee statute and Clarence Darrow, a very successful lawyer from Chicago, agreed to represent the American Civil Liberties Union (ACLU) in the defense of Scopes. Rappleyea had won for Dayton a level of public recognition far beyond his dreams. The nature of the case, the widespread anti-rhetoric against evolution, and the prospect of seeing Bryan attack evolution in a public court, was of interest all over the country. There were so many visitors in town when the trial began that some of the sessions had to be held out of doors in the blistering heart of a southern summer. A carnival atmosphere developed as people took advantage of the occasion to mount posters showing monkeys swinging from trees. There was an assumption that the trial would be about human origins because so many questions had focused on whether or not humans came from monkeys. In later years the name Monkey Trial was the one most frequently used whenever Dayton and its story were recalled.

Everyone assumed that Scopes would lose. Dayton was as fundamentalist as any place in America. It would be hard to find one person who did not subscribe to the literal interpretation of the Bible. It was from such people that a jury would be chosen. H. L. Mencken, the most prominent newspaperman, book reviewer, and political commentator of his time, wrote a scathing review of the process, mocking anyone and everyone who thought that the minds of these fundamentalists of upland Tennessee could be changed. In his reports to the press of New York he insisted that the trial could not realistically be reported in print. It had to be experienced. The noise was more important than the logic. At the end of each session he said that the morons in the audience just hissed. Mencken's sharpest thrusts were directed against Bryan whom he called that old mountebank. He described him as having the hillbillies locked up in his pen. He could see Bryan's brand on them and they were the ones, like folk from remote hills and forlorn farms, who constituted his chief strength. In his summary of Bryan at the trial Mencken saw him as a failed politician who was now taking refuge in the consolations of these religious people. Clarence Darrow, by supporting Scopes, knew that he could not win in fundamentalist Dayton. His plan was to lose, then appeal the case to the U.S. Supreme Court where it would get national attention and perhaps a favorable outcome.

National attention was mirrored in the telegrams and messages that Bryan received from supporters. Billy Sunday, the well-known evangelist, sent a letter which included these words: "All the believing world is behind you in your defense of God and Christ and the Bible." Sunday went on in his letter to declare that evolution is the same as atheism and evolutionists are determined to eject God from the universe and destroy the Bible. Aimee Semple McPherson was the Pentecostal pastor who, in 1921, became the first person to preach a sermon by radio, using what was then called the wireless telephone. This is what she sent to Bryan from her home church in California: "Ten thousand members of Angelus Temple are praying for you in your fight for the Bible against evolution." As the trial went ahead, Bryan made the big mistake of allowing Darrow to cross-examine him. The result was disastrous for him. He was completely unable to mount a logical defense. Here is a sample of the exchange:

Q: You have given considerable study to the Bible, haven't you, Mr. Bryan? A: Yes, sir, I have tried to.

Q: The Bible says Joshua commanded the sun to stand still for the purpose of lengthening the day, doesn't it, and do you believe it? A: I do.

Q: Do you believe that at that time the entire sun went around the earth? A: No, I believe that the earth goes around the sun.

Q: Do you believe that the men who wrote it thought that the day could be lengthened or that the sun could be stopped? A: I don't know what they thought.

Q: You don't know? A: I think they wrote the fact without expressing their own thoughts.

Q: Can you answer my question directly? If the day was lengthened by stopping either the earth or the sun, it must have been the earth? A: Well, I should say so.

Q: Now, Mr. Bryan, have you ever pondered what would have happened to the earth if it had stood still? A: No.

Q: You have not? A: No, the God I believe in could have taken care of that.

Q: I see. Have you ever pondered what would naturally happen to the earth if it stood still suddenly? A: No.

Q: You believe the story of the flood to be a literal interpretation? A: Yes, sir.

Q: When was that flood? A: I would not attempt to fix the date.

Q: Have you any idea how old the earth is? A: No.

Q: The book you have introduced in evidence tells you, doesn't it? A: I don't think it does.

Q: Let's see whether it does; is this the one? A: That is the one.

Q: It says B.C. 4004. A: That is Bishop Usher's calculation.

Q: That is printed in the Bible you introduced? A: Yes, sir.

Q: Would you say that the earth was only 4,000 years old? A: I think it is much older than that.

Q: Do you think the earth was made in six days? A: Not six days of 24 hours.

Q: Do you believe that the first woman was Eve? A: Yes.

Q: Do you believe that she was literally made out of Adam's rib? A: I do.

Q: I am going to read a passage from the Bible: "And the Lord God said unto the Serpent, because thou hast done this, thou art cursed above all cattle, and above every beast of the field; upon they belly shalt thou go and dust shalt thou eat all the days of they life." Do you think that is why the serpent is compelled to crawl upon its belly? A: I believe that.

Q: Do you believe the story of Jonah and the whale, that the whale swallowed Jonah and kept him alive for three days? A: Yes.

Every visiting reporter knew that Bryan had been completely ridiculed. His supporters, however, were largely indifferent to the cross-examination because they were convinced that he would successfully counteract with his brilliant oratory. Darrow had already anticipated Bryan's rebuttal. Knowing all along that he had no chance of winning, he asked the jury to return a verdict of guilty. By the rules operating in Tennessee the jury had to agree. The trial ended and the judge awarded a fine of 100 dollars. Bryan had been denied his opportunity for a closing speech. Darrow just wanted to weaken Bryan's case through cross-examination and by preventing him responding at the end so that, if and when he appealed to the Supreme Court of the nation, he could present the defenders of the statute in Tennessee as people with a weak case. Everything had worked out pretty much as people expected. The anti-evolutionists had won and Bryan and the people of Dayton could feel happy about the outcome.

Bryan died suddenly a few days after the end of the trial. His body was taken to Washington, D.C. and he was buried in the National Cemetery because he had previously asked to be laid to rest there. Crowds gathered at railway stations all the way from Dayton to the Capital. At Jefferson City station in Tennessee a group of young men sang Bryan's favorite hymn: "One sweetly solemn thought comes to me o'er and o'er, I am nearer home today than I have been before."

In various parts of the country members of the Ku Klux Klan held memorial services for him, including the burning of crosses on each of which was inscribed, "In memory of William Jennings Bryan, the greatest Klansman of our time, this cross is burned; he stood at Armageddon and battled for the Lord." Prior to interment a funeral service was held for Bryan at New York Avenue Presbyterian Church and the service was broadcast throughout the country and Canada. The White House flag was at half-mast on that day and the State Department, in memory of his service there, was closed at noon.

One year after the Dayton trial, the Tennessee Supreme Court examined the verdict and reversed it on a technicality. The law stated that only a jury could determine a fine, not a judge. Rather than send the case back for a new trial, the Supreme Court decided to dismiss it. It felt that nothing would be gained by another trial. Darrow's plans had been foiled and everyone was surprised. A shadow had been cast over the problem of evolution, giving it, or rather its opponents, a new position of authority across the country. There was reluctance on the part of everyone to challenge laws against evolution so there was a great lull in anti-evolution activities, a lull that lingered all through the 1920s and until more immediate issues like the world depression focused minds elsewhere. This does not mean that fundamentalists were inactive but they were now active as a well-defined population within the evangelical camp. The Scopes Trial had identified them as people who were resistant to everything modern. They were the ones who hold on to the past in fixed and irrational opposition to change. They fitted perfectly into the statement I included at the beginning of chapter two.

Prior to Scopes, fundamentalism had been perceived as an urban phenomenon, supported by business and political interests, and concentrated in the older parts of America, the eastern and northern areas. After Scopes it became an integral part of rural and small-town regions of the country. One reason for this expansion was that many places and many religious groups identified with it for the first time. They had not known much about fundamentalism before 1925. Another reason was its value as a focal point for the hostility that much of rural America felt toward modern culture. Had Bryan lived on into the 1920s there might have been a very different America by 1930. His attachment to rural life would have been greatly expanded and he might have become president instead of Hoover in the dark days of the depression from 1929 onward. As it was, an obscurantist identity had been successfully given to fundamentalism, not by the outcome of the trial but by the pens of commentators and writers who contrived their various interpretations of the trial. Sinclair Lewis' successful novel *Elmer Gantry* exploited this image of fundamentalism. One writer said that, for the first time in American history, organized knowledge has come into open conflict with organized ignorance and if the latter wins we are headed back into the dark ages.

It was mentioned earlier that there was a lull in anti-evolution activities after 1925. While that was true in terms of legislative actions, it was far from true in relation to the behavior of fundamentalist organizations. In the years immediately after Scopes they reinvigorated the World's Christian Fundamentals Association and the Anti-evolution League. Friends of Bryan claimed the roles of successors and founded new organizations such as the Bible Crusaders of America to continue the fight against evolution. None of these ventures changed the picture of fundamentalism and it declined in public support. One of its big mistakes in this period of the 1920s was joining organizations which happened to be anti-evolutionist but were suspect for other reasons. For a time fundamentalists held majorities in two large church organizations, The Northern Presbyterian and the Northern Baptist. These majorities had disappeared by 1927. The strength of fundamentalism thereafter, having faded from all the large church organizations, remained within Bible schools, missionary societies, and a variety of small organizations that were linked together through magazines and conferences.

It was mentioned at the beginning of Chapter 2 that the history of fundamentalism was never a gradual development from its inception in the 19th century. Rather it flourished and faded in cycles of expansion and decay. The third of these phases has now become so strong in the early years of the 21st century, that one could call it a fourth wave of fundamentalism, one that is reinvigorated by the mirage of scientific intelligent design. For the 1920s—in contrast to all of that—it was a story of decay, but this changed in the early 1960s as a result, paradoxically, of action by the fundamentalists' arch-enemy the Soviet Union. Immediately after 1957, when the Soviet Union successfully launched its satellite, "Sputnik," the United States launched into a series of scientific projects in the hope of overtaking the Soviet Union's obvious advantage in science. One of the scientific projects was a new course in biology in which Darwin's theory of evolution would be the guiding principle all through the course. Books for teaching this new biology were distributed all across America. Fundamentalists were outraged and, as they say, the rest is history. Every thinking American has been fighting the fundamentalist mindlessness ever since.

5

Attacking Evolution in New Ways After 1960

Combine biological lessons about evolution in schools with a discussion of intelligent design.

—United States President
George W. Bush, 2005

For decades after 1925, the anti-evolution movement was relatively quiescent. There were phases of intense activity from time to time but overall there was nothing to compare with the activism of the first 25 years of the twentieth century. One thing became clear in these post–Scopes decades, fundamentalism became well known as a unique wing of evangelicalism, with an outlook that was quite different from other evangelicals. The results of all the efforts that had been attempted in *The Fundamentals* to give expression to a single united movement disappeared quickly. H. L. Mencken, who attended the Scopes Trial and wrote about·it afterward, was one of the first to declare that fundamentalism died after 1925. He thought it was no longer a significant force in American thought and culture because it belonged to the mean streets of America, the places where learning was too heavy a burden for mortal minds to carry. How wrong he was! What would he have said if he had lived to see the 2004 presidential election? Many social and intellectual developments had changed the nation between 1925 and 2004.

A martyr's mentality appeared among fundamentalists in the late

1920s and 1930s. There was a feeling among them of being part of a lost cause. Some of their leaders promoted an attitude that welcomed weakness as commendable. They should reject notions of achieving public acceptance and, instead, emulate those faithful remnants from the past, the ones who stood firm in the face of public rejection. Historians added to the myth of the demise of fundamentalism by ignoring it in their description of American society. They described it as a passing and short-lived reaction to the tide of modernism. The early battles against evolution faded away and bills that had been proposed in the early 1920s were never enacted into legislation. There were 37 anti-evolution bills introduced into state legislatures during this period that never passed into law. Textbook publishers, always sensitive to controversy, avoided the word evolution and reduced the amount of material on biology to a minimum. By default, in spite of their weakness, fundamentalists had won the battle over evolution because it had almost disappeared from the schools, but they had lost their positions in the forefront of media and in support from the bigger church denominations.

The reality of fundamentalism was not its visible image, especially its appearance in the minds of the movers and shakers in American life. Nevertheless it remained a powerful movement, still representing a large number of people with deep-rooted convictions. Their alienation from a leadership role to one of being, as it were, outsiders, carried its own popularity and respectability as so often happened with similar groups in previous times. It was a condition that strengthened their faith and boosted their sense of purpose and it happened to coincide, in the depression years of he 1930s, with developments in the Christian community at large that created a new home for them. All kinds of new groups of Christians took shape from people who had left mainline churches between 1930 and 1940. They were known as "come-outers" and they formed a variety of sects or independent fellowships. Many of these fellowships, such as The Independent Fundamental Churches of America, founded in 1930, were strongly linked together through conferences and publications so that they rivaled in size the institutions from which so many of their members had left. It was to these new places that fundamentalists gravitated and felt at home.

The Bible institutes in particular became the vital heart of fundamentalism. These places were tightly knit fellowships, dedicated to the training of evangelists, Sunday school superintendents, and foreign missionaries. By the middle of the 1930s there were about 50 of these institutes across America and some of them, as they developed established reputations, became regional training centers for religious workers. The Bible Institute of Los Angeles (BIOLA) was a well-known institute at the time of *The Fundamentals*, and came into national prominence in the 1930s as demand increased for missionary training centers. Fundamentalist pastors who held office in denominations frequently found these institutes to be much safer places than their own denominations for the training of their staffs. There was an absence of the tensions that continually surfaced in the bigger institutions. Almost all institutes arranged conferences regularly on world missionary needs or on prophecy. These conferences were open to the public. There were in addition extension departments that promoted revival meetings and Bible conferences in smaller communities. Magazines such as the *Moody Bible Institute Monthly*, various books and, by the early 1902s, radio all served to augment existing networks so extensively that institutes appeared to be in no way different from the denominations they had earlier abandoned.

By the 1940s, institutes had become for fundamentalists both homes and the centers from which local and overseas missionary enterprises were launched. The fundamentalist support of the American branch of the China Inland Mission (CIM) is a good indication of its missionary vitality. In 1930, in spite of local difficulties in China, fundamentalist institutes sent out 100 CIM missionaries. In 1936 they added 600 more. Since, by their very history, they had lost the theological schools in their former denominations many institutes added pastoral training to their programs. They also built new theological seminaries of their own, such as the California Baptist Theological Seminary in 1944. Since people with Baptist backgrounds constituted the largest number among fundamentalists, it made sense to concentrate on Baptist theological seminaries. It would not be an exaggeration to say that, in the years immediately following World War II, fundamentalism in America was very much a force to be reckoned with. It was in a strong position, ready to face new challenges. To the surprise of everyone, the challenge that did arrive and almost overwhelmed them was the same old one they had encountered in 1925, Darwin's theory of evolution.

Biological Sciences Curriculum Study (BSCS)

The story of evolution's renaissance dates from the fall of 1957 when the Soviet Union successfully launched its satellite Sputnik with a man aboard. Almost immediately there was a fear all across America that perhaps the Soviet Union had gained a scientific advantage over the West, so great that they would be able to control activities in space and possibly use space as a military base from which to attack the U.S. For months after the successful flight of Sputnik, in every coffee shop or academic classroom, people asked the same question: have we failed to keep ahead in scientific research and technology? Is it too late for America to try to overtake the Soviets? What will happen if we fail to catch up? Within two years the beginnings of a formal reaction to the crisis was in place. Congress voted very large sums of money to the National Science Foundation (NSF) for the purpose of revising and upgrading every scientific subject in the high school curriculum in order to raise both the degree of interest in scientific subjects and the levels of student achievements in those subjects. The first subjects tackled were the ones called the hard sciences such as physics and chemistry. Afterward came the biological, environmental, and social sciences.

Fundamentalists were indifferent to the work of the first two, physics and chemistry, but then a junior biology project was initiated, called "Man a Course of Study (MACOS)." It involved comparisons between animal life and human life and also between simple societies and more complex ones. The Bushmen of the Kalahari Desert and the Inuit of northern Canada were the two simple societies selected. It was not long before shocks began to reverberate among the fundamentalists. This course brought out the similarities between humans and animals. They shared many genes. The DNA was still, by 1960, a new discovery and the awareness of such close likenesses between animals and humans seemed to fundamentalists to be a denial of the narrative of Genesis. More disturbing information came from the traditional lifestyles of the Inuit of Canada, especially since the data was on film, the result of a partnership between Harvard University and the National Film Board of Canada. The details that created a storm among fundamentalists, because they were so much at variance with our values, were the practices among the Inuit in older days, such as a man borrowing another man's wife when on a long journey, in order to keep warm, and the abandonment of grandparents if they could not keep up with long walks. Euphemistically the Inuit would say they had to take grandmother or grandfather for a walk on the ice.

Protests against MACOS appeared in many places as rallies were organized against what was described as an attack on the moral character of American youth. Complaints were lodged at public meetings in schools and numerous negative editorials appeared in leading newspapers. John Dewey and all the history of progressive education were blamed for the weaknesses in science education and everywhere there were demands for a return to old fashioned chalk and talk instruction in which students were required to learn and memorize bodies of information whether or not they understood them. Yet, as the valuable findings emerged from the various NSF projects, about how to raise America's standards in science, it was Dewey's methods that were found to be the most effective. Such was the sad state of learning and achievement in science around 1960. Even the use of the phrase social science came under attack because it suggested some relationship to socialism. Questions were asked about it on the floor of Congress so, to avoid wasting time on unimportant questions, scientists changed the label social science to behavioral science. While MACOS created a lot of protest from fundamentalists it was not the main source of the explosive reactions that occurred in the 1960s because it did not deal directly with evolution. It was when the new Biological Science Curriculum Study (BSCS) was published in 1960 that serious opposition from fundamentalists began to take shape.

In the year 1959 there were extensive celebrations among the scientific community for the 100th anniversary of Darwin's famous publication and in that same year BSCS began to plan its new biology course for the upper years of high schools. A steering committee was formed at the University of Colorado, Boulder, to design the new course. It consisted of college biology teachers, education specialists, and high school biology teachers. Over a period of 18 months classroom materials were prepared by the team at Boulder, then tested out in 100 high schools across the country. As a result of these tests changes were made and the improved materials tested out again, this time in 500 schools with a thousand biology teachers. Alongside these tests summer workshops were organized to upgrade teachers' subject knowledge and to introduce them to the new BSCS course materials. By 1963 all the preparatory work was completed and three new books were distributed nationally for use in schools. They were known as the blue, green, and yellow books, each of which concentrated on a particular aspect of biology. Darwin's theory of evolution was a central theme and a guiding principle in each of the three books. In anticipation of criticism the authors of these books noted that evolution might be a new subject for some students so they should understand that, in its modern form, it is a theory that has been validated again and again for more than a century.

Two pedagogical problems faced the designers of BSCS, how to cope with the accelerated growth of biological information and how to persuade teachers to teach in the new ways demanded by the additional data. For the first of these two problems, the fact that the total amount of biological information had increased fourfold within 30 years and was expected to grow even faster in the future, the BSCS designers proposed selecting key concepts and ideas that had broad application. In other words, instead of teaching masses of discrete information teachers would select individual case studies, each representing large volumes of biological information. The curriculum would thus be manageable and the total course content could be taught. A simple illustration shows how this approach works. It relates to the theme of an organism's adjustment to a changing environment, a vital concept in evolution. Imagine trying to teach this to a very young class. A worm is placed on a sloping board and an incentive that only a worm could understand is placed at the top of the board. As the worm began to crawl upward a student tilts the sloping board to make it steeper. What happens? The worm changes its angle of ascent to make the climb easier but continues to climb. This is a very simple illustration but it defines what is meant by an idea that explains large amounts of content.

The second problem faced by the BSCS writers was the methods that teachers had been using for many years, namely helping students memorize larger and larger quantities of unrelated bits of information in order to cover the course. They saw that it would be increasingly difficult to persuade educational administrators of the value of this kind of science in the face of requests by creationists to include more important information. What was needed was a new understanding of the nature of modern science, not just the data that may or may not form part of biological research and discovery. To move teachers toward good science, BSCS writers defined all science as detective work so that classroom lessons would be consistently involved in problem solving. This would give new meaning to the nature of science. It also would fit with what we now know about the ways our brains work. The problems arising out of natural curiosity or experience require the formation of one or more hypotheses. These are tested against reality. It is only when more and more data continue to support a particular hypothesis that the term theory is used. It was through activities such as these over more than a century that the theory of evolution became an accepted part of scientific knowledge.

Forty years after its first work was completed at Boulder, Colorado, BSCS issued a revised version, *BSCS Biology: A Molecular Approach*. Its content was substantially changed to accommodate the many additions to the content of biology since the early 1960s. A new chapter dealing with advances in molecular genetics covered genomics, the Human Genome Project, mutation and DNA repair. This chapter noted that some 32,000 genes have now been identified in humans and most of them are similar to the genes that occur in every other living creature. The writers emphasize the fact that knowing an organism's entire sequence tells little or nothing about other aspects of the organism's biology, such as what the organism looks like, where it occurs, how it behaves, or how it makes its living. The writers gave a page and a half to gene therapy, starting with the declaration that the treatment or prevention of genetic defects will be the most important result of the Human Genome Project. This aspect of biology will be examined further in Chapter 7. The writers of the new BSCS warned readers of the potential misuse of genomic information about individuals. They also touched on the political aspect of science, saying this: "students who use this book will recognize that the recent debates about the regulation of stem-cell research have been wholly political affairs, even if some of the participants have been using 'scientific' rhetoric."

Reactions from Fundamentalists

Within a few years of the publication of the first BSCS books in the 1960s a rash of creationist literature appeared. There were more books on creationism published between 1960 and 1970 than in the previous 30 years. Henry Morris' book on the Genesis flood dominated this list in terms of sales and popularity. Chapter 2 mentioned that there were three phases of fundamentalist opposition to modern science, all of them in different ways determined to prevent the acceptance of evolution. This one that began with the publication of the BSCS books was the final and most extensive of the three because of the new and widespread status that had been given to evolution. Many creationists felt that their efforts over the previous decades against evolution had been a failure. Beginning in the 1960s and continuing for the rest of the century and right up to the present time, a continuous series of organizations and publications emerged, all of them dedicated to the prevention of the teaching of evolution in schools. The first was creationism, then creation science, then Answers in Genesis, and finally the so-called non-biblical, "scientific" intelligent designers. The Henry M. Morris and John C. Whitcomb Jr. book, published in 1961 by the Presbyterian and Reformed Publishing Company in Philadelphia, was little more than a revision of the earlier work and publications of the Seventh Day Adventist George Price at the beginning of the twentieth century. It was the first reaction.

Its full title was *The Genesis Flood: The Biblical Record and Its Scientific Implications*, and it stood as the voice of creationists from 1961 to 1990. Thus the flood thesis had a life of almost a century before contemporary advances in knowledge forced creationists to invent new labels for their protests. Like Price, Morris and Whitcomb Jr. discarded any idea of uniformity in geological history. In six literal days, they asserted, using methods that as yet are not understood, God had created the entire universe and populated the earth with fully-grown plants, animals and humans. Evidence was adduced that humans and dinosaurs had lived together at the same time. Human footprints alongside those of dinosaurs, even a dinosaur track superimposed on a human one had been found, they claimed. The fall of Adam and Eve, they said, had introduced decay and deterioration to a world that had been perfect. All the rock strata with their fossils had to post date this event. It all happened within the last 6,000 years. Within its first decade the book sold tens of thousands of copies and over the following 15 years an additional 150,000. Morris and Whitcomb Jr. became famous sought-after speakers and authors. Strict creationists were delighted to have a book that made catastrophism respectable while scientists scorned it. The controversy over its accuracy added more sales. Most of the evangelical journals were interested in it but few gave it their full support.

Morris visited and spoke at churches and theological colleges all over America. Many of the more conservative ones invited him to join their faculties. At Bob Jones University, where two of Morris' sons were enrolled, the administration offered to put him in charge of a new department of apologetics. At Dallas Theological Seminary, the largest nondenominational conservative seminary in the world, his lecture "Biblical Cosmology and Modern Science" was received enthusiastically with students giving him a standing ovation at the end of the lecture. Two years after the appearance of *The Genesis Flood*, Morris along with several others formed the Creation Research Society. Its statement of belief was a clear recognition of majority creationism at that time, a belief that remained strong for most of them throughout the 1970s and 1980s. Here are its five components, all of them binding on all members of the society: (1) the Bible is the written word of God, and because it is inspired throughout, all its assertions were historically and scientifically true in all the original autographs. To the student of nature this means that the account of origins in Genesis is a factual presentation of simple historical truths; (2) all basic types of living things, including man, were made by direct creative acts of God during the creation week described in Genesis. The biological changes that may have occurred since creation were only changes within the original species.

The statement of belief for the Creation Research Society continued with number (3) as follows: the great flood described in Genesis, commonly referred to as the Noachian flood, was a historic event worldwide in its extent and effect; (4) we are an organization of Christian men of science who accept Jesus Christ as our Lord and Savior. The account of the special creation of Adam and Eve as one man and woman and their subsequent fall into sin is the basis for our belief in the necessity of a savior for all mankind. Therefore, salvation can come only through accepting Jesus Christ as our savior.

As a postscript to the statement of belief there was a declaration that no publication of the society would ever advocate an old earth or geological-ages position. *The Genesis Flood* publication continued to be the standard bearer for creationists through the 1970s and 1980s even though the new name, Creation Research Society had been introduced. Later, additional variants of creationism appeared as its proponents sought to make it more acceptable to the scientific community. Creation Science and Scientific Creationism were two other labels employed. The hope was that creationism might be seen as a scientific study independently of belief in the Bible. Late in the twentieth century the Answers in Genesis (AIG) movement appeared, supported by creationists who felt that the moral basis of society would collapse if the Bible were not interpreted literally. They reflected Jerry Falwell's views.

AIG's views were very similar to those of Henry Morris, very much a part of the young earth creationists, seeing the earth as little more than 6,000 years old. The AIG outlook on Genesis is unusual in one particular respect. It takes a long view back in time, identifying in the process what it sees as a long-standing rejection by Christian leaders of biblical authority in favor of secular wisdom. As a result, say the leaders of AIG, many of the social problems we encounter today are due to this neglect of the absolute authority of the Bible. This is a view that is very popular today as seen in Jerry Falwell's writings. The conclusion of many is that without the absolute authority of the Bible, morality will disappear and there will be no law in communities other than that of the jungle. Kenneth Ham, spokesman for AIG, published a book in 1989 called *The Lie: Evolution*, based on the argument that because it cannot be made to fit his interpretation of the Bible it must be false. AIG remains today a powerful voice in America. About 500 radio stations broadcast its messages every day and these are supported and enhanced by books and videos. AIG's latest venture is the biblical museum in Kentucky, a multi-million audio-visual center, complete with three-dimensional models that illustrate the audio and visual content.

The ID Mirage

By the 1990s and early 2000s, the face of creationism was very different. It had gone through a fundamental change. No longer was the focus on an old earth and different interpretations of the historical content of Genesis. Disputes with established scientific facts had faded and several creationist leaders happily accepted the four plus billion years of the earth's age along with a much greater age for the rest of the universe. The new phrase that came into vogue and very soon became the defining label of creationism was intelligent design.

It was and is a very old idea in its essential meaning and this book has already identified it in its earlier form as William Paley's natural theology. The majority of creationists are now advocates of intelligent design. ID is a very simple idea with an age-old pedigree, the practice of including a transcendent being to explain events that are not understood. It was the approach used by hunters and gatherers, thousands of years ago, when thunder or lightning struck their world, and it was the approach used by shamans and other religious leaders when the solution of medical problems eluded them. In today's world the wealth of new things in molecular biology provides a fruitful source for the ID approach.

ID today has nothing to do with science and every time it is imposed on the science curriculum of schools, as is often the case, teachers ask the question, how do I teach this subject? The only possible answer is, tell them! That's the end of the lesson! However, because philosophers have got involved in imposing ID on schools it is necessary to review their field of ideas. Michael J. Behe is professor of Biochemistry at Lehigh University and author of *Darwin's Black Box: The Biochemical Challenge to Evolution*." He is a member of the Biophysical Society and also of the American Society for Molecular Biology and Biochemistry. The title of his book is drawn from a statement by Darwin along the following lines: if it could be demonstrated that any complex organ existed which could not possibly have been formed by numerous, successive, slight modifications, evolutionary theory would absolutely break down. Darwin was speaking about a particular mechanism that has since been discarded but, just like so many others, Behe was picking up on something that had nothing to do with the theory of evolution. He goes on to argue that the most convincing evidence for design is not to be found in the stars or the fossils, but in biochemical systems. He goes on to say that any system that is irreducibly complex is one where the removal of one of its parts causes the whole system to cease functioning. He picks the common mousetrap as an illustration of one such system. Any system of this kind, says Behe, cannot be produced directly by numerous, successive, slight modifications. Natural selection can only choose systems that are already working as complete wholes, so a biological system would have to arise as an integrated unit for natural selection to be able to act on it.

Behe's book was very popular because it seemed to cast serious doubt on the theory of evolution and, at the same time, to demonstrate the necessity of a creator, a designer of life. The Evangelical publication *Christianity Today* honored him with their book of the year award in 1997, the year after it was published. Behe was greatly influenced by the writings of other creationists but he is far removed from the leaders of the 1960s and before. He is not devoted to the idea of a very young Earth, nor is he critical of the basic Darwinian theory of evolution. He is quite happy with the concept of the universe being billions of years old and all life on planet earth having a common origin. While his book was a bestseller and was widely accepted by the community of people opposed to Darwin's theory, it was based on a view of evolution that excludes the role of a creator, a role that Darwin assumed in his theory. Darwin was by no means competent in regard to understanding the mechanisms that caused evolution. He was quite clear about the fact that all life emerged from a common origin, but the paths by which life changed were not known in his time. Unfortunately, it is commonplace today to find people like Behe who build theories on indefensible premises.

Behe is an advisory board member of the Intelligent Design and Evolution Awareness Centre in San Diego, which was established in the year 2001, and is dedicated to the priority of intelligent design theory. In his book, *Darwinism Comes to America*, Ronald Numbers quotes from Michael Behe's book and also from a subsequent interview regarding this book, indicating that Behe thought of his book as pushing Darwin's theory to the limit by opening the ultimate black box, the cell, thereby making possible our understanding of how life works. Behe goes on to say that the astonishing complexity of subcellular organic structures led him to conclude, on the basis of scientific data, not from sacred books or sectarian beliefs, that intelligent design had been at work. So Behe is anxious to separate himself from any defense of Genesis. Instead, he is saying that he has established his views on the basis of scientific data. Behe even says that the result is so unambiguous and so significant that it must be ranked as one of the greatest achievements in the history of science. This is an extraordinary and foolish statement to make since his conclusion has nothing to do with science. The best traditions of science are characterized by intellectual humility. Isaac Newton and other scientists displayed that frame of mind as they worked with real world data for their discoveries. Behe is working with undefined ideas that can neither be validated by experiments nor employed to predict anything.

It is not often possible to find religious sources that will refute the ID claims of molecular biologists. Evangelicals are particularly weak in this area as seen in the award given to Behe by the main evangelical periodical *Christianity Today*. One exception is the Vatican, where expertise in scientific matters has long been an outstanding feature of its work. In November of 2005, the Rev. George Coyne, Jesuit Director of the Vatican Observatory, said this about intelligent design: "This is not science. It doesn't belong in science classrooms. Placing intelligent design alongside evolution is wrong and is akin to mixing apples and oranges. Intelligent design is not science even though it pretends to be. If you want to include it in schools it should be taught when religion or cultural history is taught, not in science. If people respect the results of modern science and indeed the best of modern biblical research, they must move away from the notion of a designer God, a sort of Newtonian God who made the universe like a watch that ticks along regularly. God in his infinite wisdom is creating a world that reflects freedom at all levels of the evolutionary process toward greater and greater complexity. He is not continually intervening." There is much more to be said about the meaning of supernatural creative activity, a vital part of all ID arguments. This meaning is unrelated to the theory of evolution but it needs additional consideration. More will be said about it at the end of this section, but first the views of other ID advocates along with some comments from its opponents will be covered.

William Dembski is a research professor in the Conceptual Foundations of Science at Baylor University. He is also a senior fellow with the Discovery Institute's Centre for the Renewal of Science and Culture, which is located in Seattle. Dembski is a Christian philosopher of science who, along with some others, contributed to the new publication of the intelligence design people, *Origins and Designs*, launched in the 1990's. He is also the Executive Director of the International Society for Complexity Information and Design, a U.S. non-profit organization dedicated to the study of complex systems. One of the interesting aspects of Dembski's work is its separation from Christian views of the universe. He feels that many non–Christians are involved in the study of intelligent design, although his personal position is as a Christian philosopher of science. Amongst Dembski's books are the following: *Designing Science: Eliminating Chance Through Small Probabilities; No Free Lunch: Why Specified Complexity Cannot Be Purchased Without Intelligence*; and *Intelligent Design: The Bridge Between Science and Theology*. Dembski is a strong supporter of Behe's work. As a philosopher-mathematician he suggested that there are certain standards by which you can identify intelligent design. These include the consideration of contingency, which means chance, and specification, which means laws, and complexity. It is the evidence of complexity that gives strong support to the notion of intelligent design.

Like others in the intelligent design movement, Dembski prefers not to identify with the word creationism because of its many different meanings. He prefers to describe himself as a Christian philosopher of science with a particular interest in intelligent design. He believes that God created the world but he does not regard Genesis as a scientific document. He can readily accept that the Earth is more than four billion years old and that the universe is three times that age. He insists, like the scientists studied in the earlier part of this book, that science and scripture do not contradict each other. Scholars such as Behe and Dembski are at the core of the intelligent design movement and because of their scholarship credentials they attract people who would never have taken an interest in the older creationist models. Some people use the phrase the new creationism for their work, particularly because of Dembski's emphasis that non–Christians can be involved. As already seen, it is the intelligent design argument that appears most frequently among legislators who propose adding creationism to school science. Scientists are not so kind to the work of these two scholars. Richard Dawkins calls it intellectually dishonest. He thinks that a cowardly flabbiness of the intellect afflicts otherwise rational people when they are confronted with long-standing religions. Kenneth Miller, an evolutionary biologist, dismissed intelligent design as an imposter masquerading as a scientific theory.

Michael Denton is a molecular biologist at the University of Otago, New Zealand. He is not a biblical creationist and describes himself as an evolutionist. He is often regarded as the person who laid the intellectual foundations for the intelligence design (ID) movement. That may be due to his book published in 1986 called *Evolution: Theory in Crisis*. Denton regarded a book by Phillip E. Johnson, a person that will be covered later, as the single best critique of

Darwinism that he had ever read. He became deeply involved in the intelligent design movement substantially as a result of that influence. More recently Denton has also written another book called *Nature's Destiny: How the Laws of Biology Reveal Purpose in the Universe*. That book, published in 1998, took a very different view of nature and the cosmos. In Denton's mind, it is entirely what is called an anthropomorphic story. That's a term that is used when things refer specifically to human life. Denton argued that the entire cosmos is a specially designed whole thing with life and humanity as its single goal and purpose. In other words, all aspects of reality, from the size of galaxies to the boiling point of water, are designed for this one goal. The interesting thing about this anthropomorphic view of the universe is that scientists will say something similar. In their view, everything forms part of a single unity of purpose of form. They would see this unity of purpose as a natural phenomenon because human reason can look at the universe and see its coordinated whole.

Thus, rather like Dembski's view of the Bible and intelligent design, so Denton's view could be conceived as two views from different vantage points. Denton is a member of the editorial advisory board of the publication *Origins and Designs*. Like others with similar enthusiasm for intelligent design, Denton selects a view of Darwinian evolution that has nothing to do with the theory of evolution, and is not scientifically defensible, in order to make a case for ID. He stated that the essential bedrock of Darwinism is that all the forms of life that ever existed were generated by undirected mutations. Every evolutionist would reject that assertion.

Phillip Johnson, a former law professor and a conservative criminal law expert at the University of California at Berkeley, is another ID advocate. His publication in 1991, *Darwin on Trial*, gave a strong impetus to the ID movement and Johnson has remained one of its leading exponents ever since. The inspiration for his book came from reading Richard Dawkins' book, *The Blind Watchmaker*, in which Dawkins makes the comment that biological research provides good evidence for atheism. There is no excuse for that kind of statement. It's totally unjustified, and all responsible scientists would say so. Unfortunately, some scientists do overstep the mark and go beyond their field of expertise. This book of Johnson's was so successful that the Governor of Alabama sent copies to every biology teacher across the state. Later, Johnson's second book, *Reason in the Balance: The*

Case Against Naturalism in Science, Law and Education, was published in 1995 and was equally well received.

The problem with Johnson, as with so many others in ID, is that a phrase or a word is taken out of context, or is not correct in the first place, and a whole argument is built on it. For example, in the case of Johnson, he makes the statement that material entities subject to physical laws account for everything in nature. He says that scientists make that claim. He does not indicate which scientists he had in mind, perhaps because it might be very difficult to find one to support his statement. On this totally unsubstantiated statement he then proceeds to build a case against evolution. If only he had read the last words of Darwin in *The Origin of Species*, he would know how false was his basic premise: "This view of life, having been originally breathed by the Creator into a few forms or into one." Thus Johnson builds up his case about naturalistic limits of thought. The other assumption that Johnson makes in his writings is that the theory of evolution is based on Darwin's suggestion that natural selection was the mechanism that determined changes through the history of life. Now we know that Darwin was not correct in making that assumption. His expertise lay in the basic theory of evolution about the common origin of all forms of life, but he was not an expert on the mechanisms involved. Subsequently, it has been discovered there are many mechanisms affecting the transformation of life forms. People like Johnson capitalize on something that is a weakness and has subsequently been corrected but, because Darwin had written it, they feel that they can build a case on it.

Another illustration of the way in which experts tend to go beyond their field of competence is illustrated in the way that Johnson refers to the outlook of biological evolutionists. In universities and in schools of training, he says, the history of life belongs to evolutionary biology. This assignment of authority implies that the question of how living organisms came into existence is a matter of specialized knowledge, knowledge that is not available to persons outside the inner circle of science. This is quite wrong. No evolutionary biologist claims any knowledge whatsoever about the origin of life. It is this habit amongst the ID people of picking on things that are not an integral part of true science, and building a case on it, that causes the difficulties for mutual understanding. These various claims that are so unwarranted, namely that naturalism is the only legitimate way of doing science, and then going beyond the bounds of science to focus on conditions for which scientists have not expertise, such as the origin of life, is a big part of the difficulty of getting understanding between the two worlds of science and Christian faith. When the Kansas Board of Education in 1999 abolished the references to evolution and the great age of the earth, Johnson described the Board's decision as courageous. Why? Everyone knows it was a totally unsupportable decision. As a result, Johnson found himself among the political leaders of that time who supported the Kansas decision for crass political gain.

Of even greater significance was Johnson's interference with a bill going through the United States Congress, the infamous education bill, "No Child Left Behind." According to Edward J. Larson, Senator Rick Santorum of Pennsylvania—who wanted to introduce an amendment to that bill—had Phillip Johnson help him draft it. Fortunately, Santorum was unable to have his amendment entered within the bill because there were enough senators who knew a little about the theory of evolution. The amendment was added as a footnote to the bill and ever since, because of the prestige of any senate document, that note has been quoted by ID advocates in their attacks on school science. The actual wording of Santorum's addition was, "Where biological evolution is taught, the curriculum should help students to understand why this subject generates so much continuing controversy." In recent years, several states have been presented with ID bills proposing shared treatment of creationism and evolution, and in each case the Santorum note is adduced for support.

Very few creationists realize that leaders like Dembski and Johnson, unlike Darwin, are opposed to a Christian view of creation. They insist, especially Dembski, that their designer must not be supernatural because they want to show that the whole basis of ID is a scientific argument and therefore restricted to what can be found in observed phenomena. By taking this position, and Dembski has done so again and again in his writings, the designer must exist within nature. That means pantheism, a religious view that is totally rejected by evangelical Christians. Does President Bush know that by advocating ID as a supplement to the science curriculum of schools he is encouraging young people to believe that the one who created nature and natural things lives inside nature? According to IDs, he or she or it can be found in any blade of grass, in any animal, or in any person.

Two terms are never defined in the various discussions about ID and evolution, the meaning of the phrase "The theory of evolution" and the meaning of the word "design." The theory of evolution means one thing, and one thing only, the descent through time of all forms of life from one or two simple originals, yet invariably, IDs propose their theory on the basis of one of the many mechanisms involved in these life changes. For Behe, Dembski and Johnson, this was true and furthermore, the mechanism they selected—naturalism—is no longer regarded as very important. Design is the other thing that needs to be defined. In modern society it means conceptualizing something so that someone else can fabricate it, yet all the ID literature refers to design in the old-fashioned way, the way of Paley's watchmaker in which conceptualizing and fabricating was done by the same person. Howard J. Van Till, an evangelical Christian and a professor of physics and astronomy, points out that this view of ID implies an interventionist designer. He says that IDs envisage some supernatural designer who does his creative work by an ongoing series of discrete actions involving the micromanagement of the details of nature. This, in Van Till's mind, is contrary to evangelical thinking about creation. It is also at variance with what was quoted above as the viewpoint of the Vatican. For evangelicals who view IDs as supporters of biblical truth, this understanding of their creator must be as scary as Dembski's pantheism.

ID and the Dover School Board

The experience of the Dover School Board in Pennsylvania during 2005 is a good illustration of the triumph of common sense about science over mindless fears and prejudices. The state of Pennsylvania happens to have one of the best United States curriculum guides for high school biology but, as often happens across the country, individual school boards, under pressure from parents, add to or subtract from the approved curriculum in order to prevent the teaching of evolution. Dover was the first United States school board to add intelligent design to the biology course in order to weaken the content on evolution. It turned out to be a prescient move because later in 2005 the President, George W. Bush, endorsed the idea of adding intelligent design to the biology course. Soon, all across America, school districts began to wonder if they too should add intelligent design to their biology. The media picked up the details and it became a national and international story. Several European and Asian countries started discussions on what they thought was a new science.

In their misguided understanding of Darwin's theory of evolution, the Dover school board instructed its superintendent, against the wishes of the teachers, to introduce the curricular change by reading to the biology class the following statement:

> Because Darwin's theory is a theory, it is still being tested as new evidence is discovered. The theory is not a fact. Gaps in the theory exist for which there is no evidence. Intelligent design is an explanation of the origin of life that differs from Darwin's view. The reference book *Of Pandas and People* is available for students to see if they would like to explore this view. As is true with any theory, students are encouraged to keep an open mind.

The school board had on hand 50 copies of *Of Pandas and People: The Central Question of Biological Origins* that had been donated anonymously. There is no mystery about either the contents of this book or the purpose for which the school board added it to the course materials. The National Center for Science Education (NCSE) knew about it from its date of publication in 1989.

It is a small book of six case studies in which the evolutionary point of view and the ID one were placed side by side. The intention was that schools could give space to both views of the origins of life and decide, in the process, which was the better. Predictably, the ID seemed to come out ahead every time, and it was not long before the few schools that were using the book lost interest in it. To the directors of NCSE the fact that it dealt with origins of life convinced them that the purpose for writing it had nothing to do with the theory of evolution, a theory that does not deal in any way with the origin of life. NCSE could see from its day of publication that it was a creationist plot masquerading as a scientific book. It was the first book to use the words intelligent design in the hope, like many others who later used the same phrase, that the book would be treated as being scientific and completely independent of creationist thinking. A glance at the following quote from the book is usually sufficient to show that the real purpose of the authors was to confirm the literal historical accuracy of Genesis chapter one: "Intelligent design means that various forms of life began abruptly through an intelligent agency, with their distinctive features already intact, fish with fins and scales, birds with feathers, beaks and wings, etc. Some scientists have arrived at this view since fossil forms first appeared in the rock record with their distinctive features intact, rather than gradually developing."

Fortunately, not all of the parents in Dover thought that pandas and people was the best intellectual fare for their sons and daughters. Even within the school board there was dissension because the decision to introduce intelligent design was only passed by a 6 to 3 vote. By the beginning of September 2005, as the new school year was beginning, nine parents launched a court action against the school board. They claimed that a religious theory was being inserted in a school district's curriculum with no concern whether it had scientific underpinnings. They claimed that the board was doing what anyone would do if he or she wanted to incorporate a religious point of view in a science class and cared nothing about its scientific validity. Perhaps the school board was thinking back 80 years to the famous Monkey trial of 1925 when creationists won because of a legal technicality. In November of 2005, at local elections, eight of the nine members of the Dover School Board were ousted and, a month later, the court judgment came down. It was a thorough rejection of any attempts to include intelligent design in biology. See Appendix C for details.

Intelligent Design and William Paley

This book mentioned in the introduction that advocates of intelligent design base their thinking on the writings of William Paley (1743–1805) whose great work on natural theology began with a story about finding a watch while out walking. See drawing on page 132. The ID people of today go beyond watches to models from molecular science in order to prove the existence of a great designer. Unfortunately for them they chose the wrong model to emulate in their attempts to prove the existence of an intelligent designer. While it is true that Paley wrote about proofs of a creator, the thesis in his natural theology—as in his work on "evidences"—had nothing to do with proving the existence of God. In Paley's day and in the lifetimes of all the great scientists before the middle of the nineteenth century, the existence of God was never in question. For them, all research on and writing about nature was done in order to reveal the character of the creator. This was what Paley wrote in order to dispel any thoughts that he was trying to prove the existence of God: "For those

William Paley in his book on natural theology said that someone finding a watch would learn a lot about the person who made it. He then went on to say that, similarly, the intricacies of natural things reveal a lot about the Creator's character.

who might read my work in order to prove the existence of a God they end up where they began because they were never ignorant of God's existence. Thus nothing is gained from such researches because no proofs were ever required."

Just as Paley worked with a firm conviction about the existence and activities of a creator, so did all the great scientists of his time and those before him. Isaac Newton studied his Bible daily, believing it was true in every way. All through his life he tested scientific findings against biblical truth and never found any contradictions between them. He devoted enormous amounts of time to biblical research, including an extended examination of the dimensions of Solomon's temple. He even proposed that God must have done a special miracle when a friend of his was unable to match his research with biblical statements. James Hutton, the founder of geology and the person who first discovered the great age of the earth, saw all of his research as work inspired by his love of the Bible and by his desire to find out all he could about his creator. As he developed his theory of a self-renewing earth through cycles of erosion and rebuilding, he concluded that this was the creator's way of maintaining the earth's resources for humanity. Charles Darwin was equally devoted to his Bible and to the activities of his creator. He spent a lot of time studying books about the Bible because he was unhappy about the interpretations he had been given by Anglicans. He concluded, wrongly as it turned out later, that changes in life forms over time happened through fixed natural laws.

IDs experience trouble at every turn in their attempts to prove the existence of the great designer. He, she, or it cannot be supernatural because they want to show that they are presenting scientific evidence and they know that such must be natural. However they are unhappy with the scientific world because it limits the definition of natural to material things like rocks, climate, and living things. They want to enlarge the meaning of natural so they can demonstrate the existence of the great designer but even with a broader definition of natural they still cannot find testable hypotheses. Paul Davies, the Australian scientist, points out that using the idea of irreducible complexity as an argument is useless because, in science, complexity becomes reducible all the time as new discoveries are made, so the need for the great designer disappears in time and ID becomes an anti-god theory. IDs, just like all who work in science need to heed the advice of Francis Bacon, the 17th century writer: "Search diligently as far and as diligently as possible in the book of God's word and in the book of God's works. Then beware that you do not unwisely mingle or confound these discoveries together." Paley used the word revelation in his writings to make it clear that he regarded origins and undetectable things as being in one domain of knowledge that was not subject to scientific inquiry while the world we encounter every day could be investigated by science to provide a different domain of knowledge.

The vagaries of ID science received a gentle rebuke in 2005 from Eric Cornell, the winner of the Nobel Prize for Physics in 2001. Cornell asked the question, why is the sky blue? He gives two possible answers to his own question: (1) because blue is the color that God wants it to be and (2) because of the wavelength dependence of Rayleigh scattering. Cornell is an expert on Rayleigh scattering and he pointed out that before we understood this particular optical phenomenon there was no scientifically satisfactory explanation for the sky's blueness. In response to his first suggested answer to the original question, Cornell said that the idea about God wanting it to be was a correct answer before scientists came to understand Rayleigh scattering and it continues to exist today not in the least undermined by our advances in scientific understanding. The religious explanation according to Cornell has been supplemented but not supplanted by advances in scientific knowledge. Cornell went on to comment on intelligent design because it was in the news at the time. He said that the central idea of ID is that nature is the way it is because God wants it that way, an interesting idea that could be pursued in theology but a boring idea in science. He added that, in 1855, no one told the future Lord Rayleigh that the scientific reason for the sky's blueness was that God wanted it that way; fortunately, if people had said that to him, he was smart enough to ignore them. For science, intelligent design is a dead-end idea.

6

Interpreting the Bible

There is more ado to interpret interpretations than to interpret the things.

—Michel De Montaigne, 1580

Long before the time of Michel De Montaigne the so-called Christian world of Europe was embroiled in biblical interpretations, a consequence of the Bible being copied and distributed in larger numbers than any other book in the history of the written word. Throughout its long life, new languages, new language usage, and errors in copying all contributed to endless debates over the right interpretations of particular passages. For a thousand years after the time of Christ, people were better acquainted with interpretations than with the biblical text, mainly because there were far more interpretations in libraries than copies of the Bible. It was probably safer to read interpretations anyway because, at that time, your life might be worth nothing if you decided to interpret the Bible in a way that did not agree with the official interpretations of the church. Interpretations of the Bible lie behind every one of the anti-evolutionism movements of the past century. From flood theology, through creationism, creation science, Answers in Genesis, and now intelligent design (ID), the defense of particular biblical interpretations—all of them opposed to the theory of evolution—defined to a large extent the purpose of each movement.

The Earliest Interpreters

If one goes back to the beginnings of Christianity, one finds that the earliest interpreters of the Bible, the ones who lived in the first few centuries after the time of Christ, developed methods of interpretation that are still in use today. One of these, shaped in large measure by Jewish thinking, saw everything as symbolic. (Modern folk tend to use words like "simile" or "metaphor" instead of "symbolism.") This approach at the beginning was to be expected since most of the first generation of Christians had their roots in Jewish culture, a culture that was accustomed to this method. Alexandrian scholars such as Clement and Origen promoted symbolism because it was a very convenient approach for two reasons: it defined the Bible as a single book consisting of both new and old testaments, not two independent books, and it avoided having to make sense of the original meanings of Old Testament events. The easiest way to describe the method is to give examples. One, taken from Origen's writings, compares the narratives of the book of Joshua in the Old Testament with the gospels of the New Testament. Joshua's conquest of the land is then described as symbolizing Jesus' conquest of sin on the cross. There were excesses in the use of this method, as interpreters tended to read any meaning they liked into biblical passages, but in time consensus developed over what was defensible and what was not.

It is easy for one to think that this approach to interpretation makes no sense but, if one looks at the Bibles of today, one can see many examples of this same method being employed by the New Testament writers. Paul refers to a rock in the wilderness during the wanderings of the Israelites as representing Christ. The gospels record a statement by Jesus in which Jonah's three days in a whale symbolize his three days in the grave. This particular simile, because it was tied to the words of Jesus, persisted for a long time. Illustrations in a 12th century Bible depict the two events together, Jonah coming out of the whale at the bottom of the picture and Jesus rising from his grave above it. Long before the 12th century, the dark ages of an authoritarian church had taken control of all interpretations and determined which ones were to be the right ones. Any person who dared to propose alternatives during that long thousand-year period had to face the torturers and death unless he or she recanted. Often, today, it is difficult for people to feel sufficiently free of the influence of that past to tackle biblical interpretation in the light of present knowledge.

Other interpreters from the ancient past, especially those in the place known now as Turkey, saw the Old Testament as having meaning in its own right with content that applied to particular people in their own locations. At the same time they saw secondary meanings that applied to Christ. These prophetic and symbolic approaches also stayed with biblical interpreters right down to the present time and are still in use but the way they were and are employed has changed. Greek influences in Christian thought, especially those of Aristotle, determined the interpretations that prevailed before modern times because of the influence of Augustine, an influential leader from the western Mediterranean, who had adopted much of Aristotle's thinking. Aristotle had a philosophical view of knowledge that encompassed the entire universe wherein natural objects had significance only as symbols of biblical interpretations. Rocks and plants and birds were treated like verses in the Bible, things to be interpreted as illustrations of Christ. A pelican was a symbol of Christ's suffering, for example, so even today representations of pelicans can be found in European cathedrals. Thus the totality of all knowledge was related to biblical interpretations. Over the centuries people came to understand that information about nature and the Bible represented two fundamentally different kinds of knowledge and each needed to be studied differently and independently.

Galileo Galilei (1564–1642)

The well-known experience of Galileo when he interpreted the Church's understanding of the Bible differently is a classic example of the problems associated with new biblical interpretations prior to the 16th century. His name puzzles some people. He seems to have the same surname as his first name and that is true. It was a local custom. We often forget that surnames are relatively recent developments in the long stretch of human history. His home was Pisa, now best known as the place where the leaning tower stands and where special efforts were recently made to prevent the tower leaning any further from the vertical. Galileo was the oldest of a poor family of seven. He lived in Pisa for 10 years then, when his family moved to Florence, he spent several years in a monastic order as a novice before returning to the University of Pisa in 1581 to study. He was very interested in mathematics and philosophy during his years of study in Pisa. In 1585, after failing to obtain a scholarship that would enable him to continue, he had to leave the university without a degree.

One of the stories that circulated about him (it is not known if it was a true story) tells of his behavior in 1583 while attending church services at the Cathedral of Pisa and the movements of a hanging lamp caught his attention. Galileo was always fascinated with mechanical devices so his sudden interest in the lamp would not have been unusual. Perhaps the sermon was less than interesting and there was time and opportunity to concentrate on other things. He noticed that the lamp above the altar sometimes swung from side to side a small amount and at other times a lot, depending on the strength of the breezes that entered the cathedral through cracks. He decided to time the swings and, since there were no instruments in his day for measuring time, he used the pulse beat of his blood as measured in his wrist to estimate time. To his surprise the swings always took the same amount of time whether the lamp took a short or a long sideways movement. He followed up on this experience by designing a simple pendulum, arranging different lengths of arc for its swings, using different lengths of rope for the pendulum, and changing the weight of the pendulum. The outcomes were extraordinary even although Galileo did not realize their implications at the time: first, times of swings were independent of length of arc, second, times of swings were independent of size of weights on the pendulum, and third, times of swings changed when the length of the pendulum was changed. He had discovered the first accurate measure of time in all of human history. Prior to this finding no one knew how to measure time exactly. All that was known amounted to daily movements of the sun and the approximate measure of an hour using the time taken by sand to drop through an hourglass.

Galileo's fame as a scientist became known when he challenged Aristotle's long-standing theory about falling objects. Like so many of Aristotle's theories this one was not based on experimental evidence but, because of his great influence in the church over such a long time, no one had questioned his views on falling objects, that is to say no one until Galileo did. Once again, the narrative relating to how Aristotle's theory was overturned may be apocryphal, but the truth of Galileo's claim is not. Aristotle's theory was that all objects fall to the ground at a rate that is directly proportional to their weight. Galileo took a feather and a large stone to the top of the tower of Pisa and released them at the same time in order to prove that all objects fall at the same rate, no matter what weights they have. The experiment at Pisa was not successful because air resistance made the feather behave like a parachute. Galileo was completely convinced of the truth of his theory in spite of his failure to demonstrate it in his lifetime so doubt lingered for a long time about it. In the course of NASA's missions to the moon someone suggested that Galileo's theory should be tested out there because there would be no air resistance to interfere with it. This was arranged so in 1971, astronauts David Scott and Jim Irwin, during an Apollo mission, dropped a feather and a stone from above the surface of the moon. Both reached the moon's surface at the same moment.

One of the sacred beliefs of the church in Galileo's time was that the earth did not move and that the sun moved around it. We still use language that suggests this view when we talk about the sun rising or setting. Many years before Galileo's birth, another scientist, Nicholas Copernicus, discovered that this belief of the church was wrong and that, in fact, the opposite was true. The earth moved around the sun. He wrote out his findings in some detail but, because of the power of the church and its harsh methods of dealing with heretics, he was afraid to publish his findings. He finally did publish them when he knew he was at the end of his life. Galileo knew about the work of Copernicus and wrote about it secretly to friends when he was 33 years old but, like Copernicus, he was afraid of saying anything contrary to church dogma. In spite of the many mechanical inventions he had created and, in the process, gained status as a scientist, he remained silent in the public arena. The power of the church remained a scary thing for Galileo for the rest of the his life and, latterly, he was only able to avoid the executioner by recanting his belief in the motions of the earth and restating his faith in the church's position, that the earth is immovable.

The event that contributed most to Galileo's lasting reputation as a scientist occurred in Holland when he was 44. As so often happens in scientific discovery one person develops something in one place and its value gets picked up elsewhere and often, as was the case with Galileo, with much greater utility. No telescopes had been invented by the year 1608 but a spectacle maker in Holland had accidentally arranged some lenses so that they provided significant magnification of distant objects. Galileo heard about this, found out more about it, then developed something similar. He placed two lenses into a tube of lead, one at each end. Both lenses were plain on one side but convex and concave respectively on the other sides. With this simple instrument he found that he could get a magnification of nine. After a lot of practice looking at objects nearby, Galileo began to use it skyward. It was the first time that such an instrument had ever been used for astronomical observations. Copernicus had done all of his observations and research using only natural vision. Galileo focused his new telescope on Jupiter, one of the most prominent planets and usually the brightest. It was his discovery of several planets circling around Jupiter on the nights of January 7 to 10, in 1610, that established for all time the accuracy of the earlier work of Copernicus.

Galileo was anxious to avoid controversy so he decided to hide his discovery. This is never easy in scientific circles. Sharing and critically assessing one another's work is the way that errors and poor judgment are identified. Galileo shared his work with two friends and, unfortunately for him, his information was passed on to the authorities in the church. In particular, one of his statements caused great concern: a non-literal interpretation of the Bible is essential when a literal rendering would clash with proven facts about the physical world. In previous reports of discoveries it had been common practice to assert that discoveries would always prove to be in harmony with existing biblical interpretations. Galileo's words made it clear that his discoveries contradicted the church's positions and the Pope felt he had to do something about it. He arranged for a committee of cardinals to condemn all scientific theories that clashed with the church's teachings and to issue instructions that any such theories must neither be taught nor published. When the next Pope, a close friend of Galileo's, was appointed, Galileo felt he could safely publish his work so he went ahead and did so. The result was tragic. He was placed in house arrest for the rest of his life and he escaped execution only by recanting in a public declaration of all of his errors. Galileo failed to persuade church authorities that they were wrong in their understanding of a number of things both on earth and in the skies. Nevertheless there had been a beginning of what we now identify as scientific thinking. Galileo had established that the Bible was only one source of information about the environment. There were other ways of understanding the earth and its inhabitants, each contributing to a grasp of truth. Scientific knowledge was seen as one of these. It clashed with the church's beliefs in Galileo's time and it is clashing again with churches in our time.

The Bible and World Events

The prophetic form of biblical interpretation runs through all of history from the time of Christ. It is a different aspect of biblical interpretation, compared with other kinds, because it is sharply focused on relating biblical verses to present or future world events. It assumes that the Bible is inerrant and it relies on traditional translations. The Bible is full of statements about the future and about things that might occur so there has always been occasion, or perhaps temptation, to match these statements to what is happening in the world. Here is one example from Matthew's gospel, chapter 24: "You will hear of wars and rumors of wars, but see to it that you are not alarmed. Such things must happen, but the end is still to come. " The word millenarian was the name given to those who were preoccupied with such future events. They could be found in all areas of Christendom. They formed a sort of church within the church. Their goal was to awaken the sleeping church to the imminence of judgment because they were convinced that judgment would accompany the return of Christ. It would also mark the end of any chance for salvation so hence the feeling of extreme urgency. Paradoxically, at the same time as they urged people to prepare for the return of Christ, they held strongly to a biblical prophecy that convinced them of the irreversible downgrade tendencies in society and the futility of trying to reverse the effects of sin.

The impact of prophetic interpretations on fundamentalism in America is closely tied to the work and personal influence of John Nelson Darby (1800–1882). His writings formed an integral part of *The Fundamentals.* Darby was an Irish clergyman who left the Anglican Church in the 1820s over a disagreement about its lack of faithfulness to the Bible, as he saw it. Ideas about prophecy in the 19th century centered on the return of Christ and the circumstances in world affairs that related to his coming. Darby introduced two new ideas into existing millenarian prophecies as indicated at the beginning of Chapter Two. They were the idea of rapture and the recognition of dispensations as the proper interpretation of biblical prophecy. Ammerman, in her paper on North American Protestant Fundamentalism, says that most fundamentalists at the present time would identify with Darby's form of millenarianism. She used the phrase "pretribulation dispensational premillennialists " to define them, and added some supporting quotations from the Bible such as the following to identify their biblical sources: "There will be two men in a field; one will be taken, the other left; two women will be grinding at the mill; one will be taken, the other left (Matthew's gospel). We will be caught up together in the clouds to meet the Lord in the air (First Thessalonians)." The rapture referred to the first return of Christ, a secret one in which believers would silently disappear into the sky, leaving those around them bewildered. It is in interpretations of the Bible like these that the distinctiveness of millenarians is seen. Biblical words to them do not mean that they seem to mean. Weeks become sevens of years and ancient local names become the names of some modern nation or region.

Darby's system of dispensations, later publicized by C. I. Scofield at the time of *The Fundamentals*, was as unique as his rapture. It approached every verse of the Bible as having equal value. He ignored the developments and changes to earlier parts that the prophets and Jesus had revealed. Instead, he picked seven distinct segments of the Bible, as follows, each of which in his mind represented different ways of God-human relationships: (1) Before Adam and Eve sinned; (2) Before Noah's Flood; (3) Abraham's call and life; (4) The People of Israel under the law; (5) Jesus's life among the Jews; (6) The church period; (7) The rapture. The one part of this whole scheme that made no sense was Darby's decision to relegate much of the four gospels to present and future events in the lives of Jews, so a number of Jesus' words became largely irrelevant to Christians. This system of interpreting the whole of the Bible from the point of view of one millenarian is quite different from all other prophetic writings. Scofield's Bible was the older King James Version and throughout its pages, in the form of footnotes, the various dispensational interpretations were inscribed. The Apartheid Bible that was used in South Africa was similar to Scofield's. It employed the older King James Version and footnotes were entered on its pages to justify the separation of blacks from white society. One verse from Genesis, chapter 10, was a favorite with the government: "God divided the nations in accordance with their languages and cultures."

It was his definition of the church and his emphasis on Jesus coming at any moment that most clearly distinguished Darby from other millenarians. The church in his mind was completely separate from all the groups and institutions that called themselves churches. He defined the church as something belonging to another world, a spiritual fellowship that existed independently from and unrelated to all the prophetic announcements and timetables in the Bible. It was, as he said, a great parenthesis within unfolding prophecy. It was unknown to the Old Testament writers so its existence stopped the clock of Biblical time, as it were, until it would be taken away in the first and silent coming of Christ. Once that event occurred the prophetic clock would once again be started and the events implicit in Daniel's Old Testament words plus all the predictions listed in the book of Revelation would begin to happen. Since all of these happenings were frozen in time pending the silent rapture, Darby's millenarianism became a popular, easily understood formula for Christians. Their salvation and eternal future depended on one thing only, a focus on and a preparation for the silent rapture.

The simplicity and popularity of Darby's dispensationalist approach to the Bible eclipsed those millenarians who had spent years trying to date the return of Christ. From 1840 to 1870, whenever positive or disruptive social or political events took place, one or other from their group would come up with a date. Books were written about particular dates, each defending the rationale for that particular date. A millenarian experienced failure almost every year during that period but, somehow, failures did not seem to inhibit additional ventures. In 1843 when the Evangelical Alliance of Protestants was formed in London, England, one writer published a book identifying the event as the fulfillment of Revelation chapter 14, particularly the words, "Take your sickle and reap, because the time to reap has come, for the harvest of the earth is ripe." Later, in 1951 in the U.S., this organization was renamed "The World Evangelical Alliance." Another writer identified the rise to power of Napoleon as the antichrist that the Apostle John had described. This millenarian was very unhappy when Napoleon was defeated and exiled in 1870.

Darby's answer to all who opposed his theology was that he depended only on the Bible for his views. He also said that the New

Testament was partly addressed to Jews and partly to Christians, so this additional unorthodox assertion separated him even more clearly from traditional Christianity. His popularity, especially in America, with its powerful emphasis on Christ's appearing at any moment, fitted well into a society that had been shaped by revivalists. Their words were always about coming to Christ now because there may never be another opportunity. There was one puzzling aspect of Darby's work and influence in America, especially when compared with Britain. In the latter, while there were many new fellowships known as Plymouth Brethren because of the early focus of his work in Plymouth, Darby had little influence among the major Christian denominations, perhaps because of the reputation for continual schism among the Plymouth Brethren groups. It was a completely different story in America where Darby had spent a lot of time during his many visits. There he encountered widespread acceptance among mainline churches, much more extensively than with the few American Plymouth Brethren fellowships that arose, but there was a catch in their acceptance.

They had no intention of leaving their denominational connections. To Darby this was central to all of his theology and he blamed their inconsistency on their worldly condition. He said that people join churches for respectability but their lives are spiritually feeble. They love to organize and do things but as far as a life with God and a love of truth, they hardly ever even think of these things. In later years his frequent comment went something like this: they take what they want from my theological bag but refuse to forsake their positions within the denominations. Clashes were common between Darby and leaders in the fundamentalist community because denominations formed the heart of evangelical life in the 1870s. *The Princeton Review*, the strongest defender of evangelical life at this time, published in 1872 a very negative article about the Plymouth Brethren. It said that they were people who gather churches out of churches. They disintegrate thereby all existing bodies by drawing away from them the best of their members. The article went on to accuse them of prowling unceasingly around all the churches and reaping where they had not sown. On the whole Darby found greatest acceptance of his views with Baptists and Old School Presbyterians because they shared with him a strong loyalty to an emphasis on God's grace.

Origin of Inerrant in Its Original Form

As one leaves those earlier battles over interpretations and comes to the present time, there is one important statement that relates to the familiar 66 book Bible: it says that every one of these books is both infallible and inerrant in its original form. As one will see, fundamentalists mean something different from other evangelicals in their understanding of this statement, but almost all evangelicals subscribe to it. To fundamentalists it means loyalty to the way the Bible was understood in the centuries before the emergence of scientific thought and method. They see their present Bibles as perfect books.

The idea of a perfect Bible in its original form is quite new in terms of the long history of the Bible and it requires elucidation. At first glance, knowing the antiquity of the Bible, it suggests an article of faith rather than a fact of history. It thereby carries the implication that perhaps there was no human element in any aspect of its creation other than the idea of humans being used as secretaries for God. As the drawing on page 146 illustrates, this was widely believed in earlier centuries and some believed it in the 18th century. For North Americans, the origin of this important qualifier, "As originally written," dates from the work of scholars at Princeton Theological Seminary. That institution, a continuation of the New Jersey College whose president was John Witherspoon and in which theological concepts were closely tied to Witherspoon's, was founded in 1812. Archibald Alexander (1772–1851) was its first professor and president. He was loyal to the Scottish philosophy of common sense and so was his successor Charles Hodge. Because Charles Hodge's two sons and one grandson also taught in the seminary, there was a consistency to Princeton's theology throughout the whole of the 19th century.

Charles Hodge was a prolific writer and in the introduction to one of his books, *Systematic Theology*, his devotion to common sense science is clearly outlined in words like the following: "if natural science arranges and systemizes the facts of the natural world, then theology systemizes the facts of the Bible and derives truths and general principles from these facts." In their approach to biblical infallibility there is a progression of thought through the various leaders. Archibald Alexander held the traditional view of biblical reliability, namely that it is the trustworthy word of God but he did not specify the meaning of that position in greater detail. That outlook had long been the accepted view of the Bible throughout Christian history. Charles Hodge, Alexander's successor, insisted on verbal inspiration and Alexander, not wishing to be dogmatic about this point went along with Hodge's position. Later, other members of Princeton's faculty emphasized that infallibility was self-evident in the Bible itself and Charles Hodge, in a surprising variant of his position on verbal inspiration, agreed that there could be small errors in the text.

Once again, at a still later point, the pendulum swung back again to verbal infallibility through the joint writings of Archibald Alexander Hodge and B. B. Warfield. Their writing was even more extreme regarding the inerrancy of the Bible than that of any one before them.

Biblical commentators in the tenth and eleventh centuries were ofter represented in art as passive listeners with the Holy Dove dictating the words of God directly into their ears.

Warfield said that if a single error could be found in the text of Scripture, then all of our teaching would be contradicted as would Scripture's own claims to be inspired. At an earlier point of time than these writings of Hodge and Warfield, this same Hodge had reaffirmed the verbal inspiration of the Bible in a book titled *Outlines of Theology*. It was published in 1860 and was popular. Charles Haddon Spurgeon, in England, used it as a text in his training of future pastors. It was republished in a revised form in 1878 and it was here that the momentous addition, "verbally inerrant in the original autographs" appeared for the first time. Archibald Alexander Hodge (1823–1886) had made his mark on biblical history thereby. Princeton's theology had now come to its final fruition. Subsequent articles in the *Princeton Review* of 1881 elevated the addition of the original autographs to a place of prominence in the Princeton doctrine of inspiration. Today it remains as one of the main doctrinal beliefs of evangelicals in both Britain and America. There was a reason for the inclusion of original autographs in the 1878 edition rather than in the 1860 one. A rash of discoveries of ancient documents in Mesopotamia, beginning with Smith's discovery in 1872, together with the recognition of errors by critics, had upset notions of Biblical inerrancy and some rearguard action was needed.

Infallibility and Inerrancy

The qualifying statement that the Bible is inerrant in the original manuscripts is of little value to the fundamentalists, the people about whom this book is written, because they see their present Bibles as infallible. Other evangelicals see things differently because they know that their Bibles have copy errors. In the years that followed the establishment of Christianity as the official Roman religion, interpreters of the Bible (the experts that are remembered as the fathers of the church), always treated the Bible as a perfect document. Only in modern times, as archeologists unearthed ancient copies of parts of the Bible, did it become clear that many mistakes had been made. Thousands of these copies, usually pieces of larger sheets of papyrus, were discovered in Egypt because the dry climate of that country protected them from decay. Some of the errors that were noted were due to mistakes; others were the result of copyists deciding that a word or phrase was wrong because of what they believed, so the manuscript was changed.

This book's introduction mentioned that science often has its own style of language usage. At times it uses everyday words that mean something quite different from the dictionary definition, so readers of scientific reports need to be aware of this to avoid misunderstandings. It is a similar situation in theology. Some theologians use the words infallibility and inerrancy with reference to the Bible but they do not mean what the Oxford dictionary says are the meanings of these two words. This dictionary says that infallible means incapable of error, that error means mistake, and inerrant means infallible. For ordinary people therefore the use of these words implies a perfect Bible, the Bible that people felt they had a thousand years ago and the one that fundamentalists are sure they have today. While the vast majority of North American evangelicals, both fundamentalists and others, subscribe to the following article of faith, they do not all agree on what it means so there is a need here to do what Montaigne spoke about so many years ago, interpret the interpreters: "The 66 canonical books of the Bible as originally written were inspired of God, hence free from error. They constitute the only infallible guide in faith and practice."

In order to distinguish fundamentalists from other evangelicals, one needs to do two things, first examine what "as originally written" really means and then investigate the understandings of infallible and inerrant as used by the outstanding scholars of evangelicalism who would not claim to be fundamentalists as this book has defined that word. The claim that once upon a time there existed manuscripts with no mistakes in any one of them, for each of the 66 books, is a statement of faith, not fact, since no one has ever seen any one of these originals. Were these original writers, then, human like the rest of us? If so, despite the quality and clarity of the inspiration they received, mistakes would be made in the recording of it for posterity just as later interpreters make mistakes in the things they did, that is unless their human personalities were bypassed and they became automatons like tape recorders. Many of the art forms of medieval times depict the biblical writers in this way. It must have been a view that was held by many at that time. It is not a view that thoughtful readers of the Bible would accept today because the Bible carries its own descriptions of the failures and mistakes that were made by many of the people whom the Bible identifies as original authors.

J. I. Packer, one of evangelicalism's best-known scholars, wrote about the meaning of evangelicalism in the 1950s because the work of Billy Graham had created a lot of public debate over fundamentalism. At that time this word was being used in Britain to define anyone who subscribed to the evangelical statement of faith. American fundamentalism was recognized as being different but the nature of the difference was unclear. There was a need for a clarifying document. This book includes some of the things that were said and written at the time. A good deal of it dealt with the meanings of "infallible" and "inerrant" and one of J. I. Packer's first observations was that the two terms have been used in so many ways by so many Christian leaders over time that it is difficult to define them today. He then went on to create general statements about their meanings, precisely the kinds of interpretations that may well be in keeping with the convictions of evangelicals but not clearly related to the actual words used. Infallible meant never deceiving or misleading and inerrant meant wholly true. These statements about the Bible may be quite accurate but they do not mean the same as saying it has no mistakes or errors. For non-specialists, including the vast majority of churchgoers, this interpretation of interpretations is very difficult to understand.

Definitions of infallible and inerrant were further extended by adding the following: the infallibility of Scripture is simply the infallibility of God speaking and biblical inerrancy and infallibility are just the confession of faith in the divine origin of the Bible and the truthfulness and trustworthiness of God. Further observations included reference to the local situations within which the Biblical authors worked. They wrote about God and their experiences using such modes of speech as were current in their days and in the common language, often presenting truth in poetic, imaginative, and symbolic forms. From all of this it is perfectly clear than infallible and inerrant do not apply to the words seen and read in Bibles today. Interpretation is needed to make sense of what is written and what is the intention of the authors behind the words. This, as already said, is irrelevant to fundamentalists who have the Bibles that the ancients had, which need no interpretation. For other evangelicals and all who try to understand the words they read in their Bibles, interpretation is essential, but the words that interpreters use must mean what the norms of language usage say they mean. It is all right to use specialist language if one is writing for specialists only. The trouble is that most books about the Bible are also read by non-specialists, so Alice's usage of language should not apply: "When I use a word it means just what I choose it to mean, neither more nor less."

Infallible Words

One of the contributors to *The Fundamentals* (see Appendix A), L. W. Munhall, in his chapter on inspiration, says this: "The words composing the Bible are God-breathed. If they are not, then the Bible is not inspired at all since it is composed only and solely of words." He then goes on to quote some others. Here is one such supporting statement, "The line can never rationally be drawn between the thoughts and the words of Scripture. We have an inspired Bible and a verbally inspired one." The writer then adds that his statements only apply to an original infallible Bible and points out that all the Christian leaders from the first few centuries held this view. These views of course are held today by fundamentalists but they are also, as seen in the discussion of infallibility and inerrancy, the conviction of many other evangelicals. How do these other evangelicals define verbal inerrancy? Can the words used mean their commonly understood meanings? As seen earlier, interpreting and therefore understanding the Bible will be possible only when there is agreement on the meanings of the words employed. This book will be quoting from the writings of outstanding evangelical theologians from the mid–20th century whose views may have subsequently changed. This may not be important, as the purpose of this book is to trace the roots of the destructive views that fundamentalists hold at the present time.

Here are some of the things that these mid-century scholars were saying. Truth that is incapable of being expressed in language is a contradiction in terms. If inspiration had nothing to do with words it would be irrelevant. One went on to say that it is verbal inspiration that assures one that the truth one possesses is valid. Another said something similar by affirming that an inerrant, infallible, revelation was given to humanity in the original words of the Bible. Others said similar things in the course of the past century yet they must have known, just to take one example, that cuneiform clay tablets were the only records of events that could have documented Genesis chapters seven and eight, and cuneiform tablets cannot be equated with language as understood today. Furthermore, even in later times, translations from one language to another were only possible by the device known as paraphrasing. To suggest that some unknown words, at some unknown time, constituted the infallible content of an initial communication from God is no help as one attempts to interpret the Bible. Nor is one helped by the extraordinary sentence from a mid-century evangelical scholar, "Truth that is incapable of being expressed in language is a contradiction in terms." What on earth does a writer mean by such a statement? What is truth to him or her?

There are many other evangelicals who hold the same statements of faith as fundamentalists and they like those met earlier interpret the words differently. Quoting one more at some length will make it abundantly clear that there has been as much confusion over the meaning of infallible words as one has seen in the cases of infallibility and inerrancy. The language in this case defines the meaning of the Bible as a God-given message set down in writing in God-given words. The definition continues to describe the Bible as the word of God written. The inspired book becomes a literary product, a verbal expression of God's thoughts, so that what is written in the Bible is the same as the thoughts of God. It is a small step from such a view of God to an idea that was quite popular among evangelicals 80 years ago. It is known as propositional revelation and it affirms that God's revelation to humanity consists of two things, actions and what is termed "words of God," the two being inseparable. Given the enormous difficulties experienced in trying to explain anything in words, attempts to be precise about the meaning of God–given words, say in English, are likely to be equally frustrating. With so much confusion among their fellow evangelicals, it is little wonder that fundamentalists stick to the old ways. They can claim to be in a tradition that goes back to the times of Paul and Peter, one that has stood the test of time. It's a safe—even if it's a mindless—position.

Conflicts over Christian Institutional Loyalties

There is one aspect of the differences between fundamentalists and NFs that is rarely discussed. It is the role of institutional loyalties. For most of the past 2,000 years, there was no such thing as freedom to oppose the teachings of the church. The particular interpretations of the Bible held by the church's hierarchy were imposed on all with the same strictness one might see in the worst dictatorships. While the old power of the church is no longer present, a variety of institutional Christian structures do exist, each with its own system of biblical interpretations and rituals. Loyalty to these institutions, some like the Roman Catholic Church and the Anglican Communion organizations of long standing, can conflict with individual or group beliefs. John Stott, who is a loyal member of the Anglican Church, stresses separatist ecclesiology as an unfortunate feature of fundamentalism because of the values he attaches to his particular Christian institution. What happens when science discovers something about nature that conflicts with the teachings of a particular Christian institution? Can those involved recognize that scientific truth in its own domain is equal in value to biblical truth in its domain? People know what happened when there was a conflict of this kind in the life of Galileo. Will the Christian world be able to do a better job with the present equivalent, the rejection by some churches of the theory of evolution?

The Roman Catholic Church (RCC), because of its age, presents more problems to thoughtful people among its members than do other Christian institutions. The strange rule about priests not marrying, for example, led to far too many cases of sexual abuse across America as well-meaning young men found themselves unable to maintain their vow of celibacy. Why impose such an unhealthy lifestyle on people when it is quite clear that marriage was the normal pattern among the early disciples, notably with Peter, the man the RCC claims as its founder? Sometime in the two or three centuries after the crucifixion of Christ, this church must have decided to institute a limitation on the freedom of its leaders. The RCC is one of the most enlightened of all Christian institutions regarding Darwin's theory of evolution. The only oddity in their full acceptance of it is their insistence that God has to inject a soul into every zygote. With such awareness of the power of reproduction in the history of life, one would think that the RCC would have made special efforts to safeguard its expression among the church's priests. There is another ancient custom in the RCC that is now being reassessed. It relates to infants who may have died at a very early age and therefore were not baptized. These day or week olds are therefore stuck with original sin, says the church, so they have to go to some afterlife limbo. They cannot go to heaven because they were not baptized. Can you imagine that any rational person would accept such an inane rule? Yet it has remained RCC doctrine for most of the church's history.

Dyson Hague, in Volume One of *The Fundamentals*, strongly opposes the findings of the higher critics because their conclusions would destroy institutional statements of faith:

> It threatens the Christian system of doctrine and the whole fabric of systematic theology. They claim that the science of criticism has dispossessed the science of systematic theology. Up to the present time any text from any part of the Bible was accepted as a poof text for the establishment of any truth of Christian teaching, and a statement from the Bible was considered an end of controversy. The doctrinal systems of the Anglican, Presbyterian, Methodist, and other churches are all based upon the view that the Bible contains the truth, the whole truth, and nothing but the truth. The 39 articles of the Anglican Church are based on this. All Scripture was

received by the great builders of our theological systems with an unassailable belief in the inspiration of its texts.

It seems clear from Hague's statements that individual or small group disagreements with, say, long-standing evangelical church beliefs are wrong. In such cases, says Hague, the church is right. That was how it used to be a thousand years ago. How can there be growth and progress if Hague is right? Perhaps the answer lies in recognizing that statements of belief by churches are almost always interpretations of the Bible, not statements about the truth of the Bible.

At an early stage in the history of evangelicalism a big problem arose between individual convictions and the established position of the Anglican Church as enshrined in its articles. I referred to it in chapter 2. It was the only major nineteenth-century theological issue that arose among evangelicals but it was a big one and it was never adequately resolved. In the Anglican order for baptism a child is declared to be regenerate at the end of the ceremony. This position was heresy to evangelicals who insisted that no one could be regarded as regenerate without the individual making a conscious decision of surrender to Christ and such a decision could obviously not be taken by an infant. J. B. Sumner, an Anglican leader who later became Archbishop of Canterbury, proposed a compromise as a solution to the heresy: he said that baptismal regeneration meant something less than becoming a Christian. He did not define what it did mean, nor did he change the wording in the order for baptism, so the problem persisted and is still present today. This, unfortunately, is typical of the double meanings that I have described above in relation to statements of faith. They occur when church leaders try to accommodate the concerns of individuals and small groups while remaining loyal to their institutions. The outcome in the minds of readers is frequently read as duplicity rather than truth seeking.

The latest conflict over biblical interpretation has a particular relevance to the RCC and the Anglican Church although it applies also to many other church organizations. It relates to homosexual activity and the reason I singled out the two oldest denominations is because the issue is particularly acute in these institutions. This conflict is not a difference of opinion over an interpretation but rather a crisis over the threat that homosexual behavior poses to the unity of the church. It seems that sexual sins rate more highly than any others in the hierarchy of prohibitions. Church leaders are convinced that they have interpreted the Bible correctly when they added this prohibition to their rules of behavior. In all probability there would not have been a crisis if the church leadership had not been involved. Homosexual activity has been common in human society for thousands of years. In response to the crisis in the RCC, especially because it was highlighted by a series of sex scandals in the U.S., the Pope issued an encyclical in 2005 banning the future ordination of any practicing homosexual. The crisis among Anglicans came as a more direct threat to their unity because churches in the U.S. and Canada decided to ordain homosexual priests. These moves led to threats of secession from large numbers of Anglicans. One archbishop from Nigeria, in 2005, threatened to lead a secession on behalf of more than a hundred other bishops from different countries. All of them were firm in their demand that either homosexual activity among Anglican leaders had to be proscribed or they would form a new denomination.

Interpreting Genesis

The battles that people like Galileo had to fight against the church in the sixteenth and seventeenth centuries have faded into the past. No responsible church leader today would insist on defending the positions that Galileo had to contend with. It is true that fundamentalists still think in terms of a perfect book, the Bible, where words mean what they mean today and where their truth is unquestioned. Many others however are equally convinced that fundamentalists' convictions are interpretations of what is in the Bible and not defensible statements of truth, especially when it comes to examining the early chapters of Genesis. It is very difficult to convince these fundamentalists that truth is a many- sided quality that can only be applied to things or people when they are in accord with reality. Because of its subject matter and great age, the Bible is often so highly regarded that people expect it to provide information on things and events about which it knows nothing. People do the same with famous film stars and presidents of nations, expecting them to be sources of wisdom on, say, science and literature when perhaps they have no competence in these subjects. Truth is found in many fields of knowledge. For fundamentalists who have such strong loyalty to the Bible, it should mean that all truth is God's truth wherever it comes from. That, unfortunately, is not the case.

The sources for the early part of Genesis may have come from non–Jewish contexts and the compilers of the Old Testament were sufficiently convinced of their value to include them. Here and there in the Bible, reference is made to sources outside Jewish culture, so maybe this was one of those external resources. Christopher de Hamel in *The Book: A History of the Bible* points out that Israelites were defeated in their own land around the seventh century B.C. and many of them taken to Babylon as prisoners. Many centuries later, in the year 1872, a British archeologist named George Smith brought back from Mesopotamia, the part of the world known now as Iraq, a large number of ancient cuneiform clay tablets that he had unearthed. One of them that subsequently was dated as having been written at the time that the Israeli prisoners were living in Mesopotamia had descriptions of creation and Noah's Flood very similar to the Genesis accounts. There are many evangelical Christians who do not consider themselves to be either fundamentalist or extreme liberal and they readily reject claims that the early chapters of Genesis constitute history as understood today. They do value these chapters as myths or, to use equivalent words, allegories of real experiences and real events.

Typical of the ways these evangelicals would describe Genesis chapters one to eleven are statements like those in the following sentences. Notice that they are written in negative terms in order to be easily understood. The events described in Genesis, chapters 1–11, never really happened in the way that the narratives of Genesis record them as happening. It is neither true that God created each creature in the space of six days, nor that the order was as laid out in Genesis, chapter 1. The human race never did originate from a man, Adam, who was formed by the hand of God from the dust, and from a woman, Eve, built by the hand of God from a rib of the man as read in Genesis, chapter 2. Sin and death never did enter the world by the man's eating a piece of forbidden fruit at the instigation of his wife and by the temptation of a speaking serpent as Genesis, chapter 3, tells. There never was the development of agriculture, herding, music, and metallurgy as Genesis, chapter 4, says. There never was a universal flood as taught in Genesis, chapters 6–8. There never was a Tower of Babel occasioning the dividing of the nations by confounding their languages as told in Genesis, chapter 11.

It is helpful to observe how an evangelical Christian commentator who would subscribe to Darwin's theory of evolution explains the meanings of the early chapters of Genesis. The approach taken is very much like that of a scientist who is trying to make sense of new miscellaneous data from experimental work. There is intellectual humility, something totally missing from the fundamentalists who treat the Bible as if it were their personal property. Derek Kidner, a theologian from Cambridge, England, is a good example of such a commentator. He is fully convinced of the validity of the theory of evolution and he relates it to his commentary on Genesis, chapters one and two, as follows: "If, as seems likely, God initially shaped humanity by a process of evolution, it would follow that a considerable stock of near-humans preceded the first humans and it would be wrong to picture these as mindless brutes. In all probability they already had a long history of practical intelligence, artistic sensibility, and the capacity for reflection. Thus the first humans would have had as contemporaries many living beings of comparable intelligence, widely distributed over the world."

These early chapters of Genesis have been revered throughout history. The fact that people have preserved them for more than 2,000 years is an indication of their value. Theologians and biblical scholars examined the record in Genesis in detail and published their findings in the many thousands of books that occupy space in libraries today. For the most part the original record was cherished because of its symbolic value. Examples of transcendent wisdom were found there that helped illuminate later parts of the biblical record. Some churches today, like creationists, see them as historical accounts, just like any other record of past events. It is quite common to find statements in their publications like the following: God created the whole universe in six days of 24 hours each, with humankind appearing at the same time, a new species of life on earth to whom God intended to entrust global government. How does a scientist approach an ancient passage of literature like the first two chapters of Genesis? How is the approach different from that of theologians or church leaders? The answer is, the scientist will discover data that time and subsequent research have validated, while he or she will ignore the presence of other data that are not of the scientific genre. In this final aspect of biblical interpretation, this book will examine two of the narratives in Genesis from a scientific standpoint, chapters 1 and 2 regarding human origins, and chapters 6, 7, and 8 regarding Noah's Flood.

Begin with the first two chapters of Genesis with no belief that the Bible is different from any other ancient document. Chapter one opens with the statement that the earth had a beginning in time, and that its condition prior to the action of God was a formless dark void. People know today that the earth did have a beginning in time. In fact geologists are now examining records in stone that date back billions of years close to that starting time. The vast amount of dust particles that preceded the beginning could probably be described as dark and void. The claim for the agency of God is of course beyond scientific knowledge. Creationists can consider it as one of the mechanisms involved, as they do, but scientists must be careful to leave that data aside because it is not experimentally verifiable. There is one other thing that interests scientists because it fits present knowledge. It is the presence of light in the cosmos prior to the appearance of the sun. Scientists know that the cosmos had a beginning in time that predates the earth by over nine billion years and in the course of that long period of time innumerable numbers of stars shone their lights across the expanse of space.

The beauty of language, the flow and cadence of repeated phrases, and the overall simplicity of the narrative are all good reasons for its having been preserved down the ages. The writers must have been competent and clear thinkers, as capable as many of today's writers. However, the cosmic framework of mind within which they operated was altogether different from modern man's, and this greatly limits the amount of data in their writings that can be linked in any way with present scientific knowledge. One significant statement comes at the very beginning of the narrative of creation. Water is mentioned before there is any mention of life forms, and this would naturally catch the eye of any biologist. Biologists know now that water is always associated with the emergence of life. That is why scientists are spending so much effort investigating the possibility of finding water on Mars. If there is water there, then in all likelihood some form of life will also be there. It was fortuitous, or maybe it was unusual insight, that made the author of Genesis record the presence of water before there was any mention of life forms.

The first chapter goes on to deal with the appearance of the sun, moon, stars, plus a variety of life forms. Human life is not referred to in this encyclopedic overview of the entire universe or, as seems more appropriate, of some parts of the solar system. At the end of the first chapter and again in much greater detail in the second chapter the creation of humans is covered. It soon becomes obvious that the focus of the entire two chapters is the story of humanity. All the earlier detail is a backdrop for it. Apart from the mention of water before life forms are described there is nothing that can be connected from these two paragraphs with present knowledge of life forms and their evolution. Darwin's theory of evolution is well authenticated by the discoveries and work of thousands of scientists. It traces the evolution of all forms of life, including humans, from some simple original forms of life that existed billions of years ago. The mechanisms of evolution involved in the emergence of these myriads of living things is still an open question but the fact of their common origin is not. In the original waters of earth the first kind of life was found and via different mechanisms all subsequent life emerged, both the billions that are now extinct and the ones seen today.

The rest of chapter two is entirely concerned with humans. It is quite clear that the author, or authors as seems more likely, regarded the entire work of creation as having happened in order to provide a suitable environment for humans, one in which this new species would be given a dominant caretaker responsibility. One can easily connect the concept of one dominant species with what is known today. The final stage in Darwin's evolutionary process, as one might call it until one knows of a better species, is *homo sapiens*, and this species has characteristics that no other possesses. These are not anatomical features because some species that lived more than a million years earlier had almost identical body appearances and similar motor skills to those of today's humans. The unique feature of *homo sapiens*, at least in the degree in which it now exists, is human consciousness. It enables humans to understand and keep a record of the past as a species and, from that record, it equips humans to predict the future to some extent. Is there any data in all of these paragraphs that connects the narrative with places on the surface of the earth? Yes, clearly there are references to the rivers Tigris and Euphrates, the area once known as Mesopotamia, now the nation of Iraq.

Another View of Noah's Flood

Chapters 6, 7, and 8 of Genesis deal with Noah's Flood, the heart of creationists' interests for most of the twentieth century. No other aspect of the campaigns against evolution lasted so long or influenced so many people. It began with George McCready Price, a Seventh Day Adventist from Eastern Canada and a prolific writer. His first major book, *Outlines of Modern Christianity and Modern Science*, envisaged a flood that covered the whole earth and changed everything. The surface of the earth, the rocks beneath, and the aftermath all added up to a recreation of the ancient earth into the world of today. His book focused on geology, a subject he considered to be suitable for explaining all the events described in the Bible. In Adventist theology, Christian values are celebrated on Saturday because that was the law in Old Testament times. Thus Price was particularly devoted to the idea that the early part of Genesis, the record of six days, must be defended as days of 24 hours each in order to be faithful to scripture. Based on the flood, he concluded that just about everything imaginable in geology had been a consequence of that one event, an event he concluded affected the entire globe.

He explained the presence of many fossils as having been deposited in various places when the flood reshaped the surface of the earth, and he attributed a great deal of the present day surface to a huge wind that followed the flood. He saw in this one event the destruction of large forests as they were swept away with the wind and the accompanying flood, then deeply buried so that in time they would be turned into the coal and oil deposits that people mine today. He was convinced that all mountains such as the Alps and Himalayas, all of which have sedimentary rocks at their summits, were deposits laid down by the worldwide flood and later uplifted. He regarded the Earth as completely without life before the narrative found in the first few chapters of Genesis. His approach to overlapping strata in rocks was that they must have been laid down at the time of the flood. In everything that he wrote, Price saw the evolution of the earth and all it contained as having happened as described in the early chapters of Genesis. Price's earth was a very young earth.

Price had little to say about fossils and the history of life. He felt that the study of geology in the light of the Bible would explain everything. In his mind the Niagara River and the Grand Canyon were carved out by floodwaters before the sedimentary elements had completely hardened. The idea of an ice age never occurred to him. When asked about it he dismissed it as the wildest dream ever imported into science. He explained volcanic activity and earthquakes as due to the ignition of coal deposits underground. Perhaps the most imaginative part of Price's geology was his suggestion that a shift in the earth's axis released massive volumes of water from subterranean reservoirs. He may have borrowed that idea from Thomas Burnet's writings in an earlier century. His one detailed reference to fossils described them as the buried remains of animals killed in the flood. All forms of life would be distributed according to their specific gravities with humans being nearest the surface since they would have reached higher ground before they were swept away by the flood. Adolf Hitler once said that if you are going to tell a lie make sure it's a really big one. People will believe a big lie sooner than a small one. Perhaps this is why Price's theories had such a long life.

Price became well known because of his many writings, especially following the publication in 1923 of what he called his main work, *The New Geology*. He was generally regarded as the main scientific authority amongst the various groups of fundamentalist Christians. When the Scopes trial took place in Tennessee, the person who was defending creationism, William Jennings Bryan, was anxious to bring him in as an authority, but he was unfortunately in England at that time. Henry M. Morris, the most influential voice in creationism from 1960 to 1990, wrote a book with John C. Whitcomb Jr. in 1961, *The Genesis Flood: The Biblical Record and Its Scientific Implications*, published by the Presbyterian and Reformed Publishing Company in Philadelphia. It was based on Price's work, essentially an updated version of the earlier book. Like Price, Morris and Whitcomb Jr. discarded any idea of uniformity in geological history. In six literal days, they asserted, using methods that as yet are not understood, God had created the entire universe and populated the earth with fully-grown plants, animals and humans.

Evidence was adduced that humans and dinosaurs had lived together at the same time because human footprints had been found alongside those of dinosaurs. There was even a claim that a dinosaur track had been discovered superimposed on a human one. The Fall of Adam and Eve, they said, had introduced decay and deterioration to a world that had been perfect. All the rock strata with their fossils must have developed after this event and all of it occurred within the last 6,000 years. Within its first decade the Morris and Whitcomb Jr. book sold tens of thousands of copies and over the following 15 years an additional 150,000. Morris and Whitcomb Jr. became celebrities and were in demand across the country as speakers. Strict creationists were delighted to have a book that made catastrophism respectable while scientists scorned the book. The controversy over its accuracy added more sales. Most of the evangelical journals were interested in it but few gave it their full support. Morris visited and spoke at churches and theological colleges all over America. Many of the more conservative ones invited him to join their faculties. At Bob Jones University, where two of Morris' sons were enrolled, the administration offered to put him in charge of a new department of apologetics. At Dallas Theological Seminary, the largest nondenominational conservative seminary in the world, his lecture on "Biblical Cosmology and Modern Science" was received enthusiastically with students giving him a standing ovation at the end of the lecture.

The real story of the Mesopotamian flood, of which the Biblical account is a faint reflection, began to unfold in he 1950s. The United States, concerned about the dangers from the Soviet Union's submarines, launched a series of underwater explorations all over the world in order to get a better understanding of the places where these submarines operated. While examining the Strait of Bosporus at the entrance to the Black Sea, one of these underwater explorations that were being conducted by a Woods Hole research vessel discovered a deep cut in solid rock at a point where the channel was only a mile wide. The research staff concluded that enormous force must have been exercised on that part of the channel at some time in the past. As the vessel sailed into the Black Sea and picked up samples of shells at different depths along the shores of the Black Sea they made a surprising discovery: again and again, always at the same depth of approximately 300 feet, they found the empty shells of freshwater and saltwater shellfish. They knew that it was unnatural for both species of shellfish to live in the same kind of water and at the same depth so they began to search for an answer. They found it some time later when they shared their findings with another research project, a geological study of the area around the Black Sea being carried out by two geologists from Columbia University, William Ryan and Walter Pitman.

These two men had been working for years on the effects of the last ice age on the landscapes of Europe. They knew that the final phase of warming had occurred about 7,000 B.C. and that huge volumes of water must have cascaded from the melting mass of ice down from the land into the oceans. They also knew that there had been earlier phases of warming and cooling and one result of the warming had been a build up of outwash rocks and gravel at the edges of the ice fields. By drilling here and there on these outwash deposits they located one that lay north of the Black Sea. It was a large mass of rocks and gravel that had been deposited by the melting ice and this material effectively blocked the fresh water from rivers such as the Volga from getting to the Black Sea. This was why the Black Sea had become almost completely dry during the final melt phases of the ice age, as Ryan and Pitman had already discovered from their field testing and drilling. Ryan and Pitman also knew from their work that what is today the Strait of Bosporus was once a land bridge. Gradually the puzzle that began in the Woods Hole research vessel began to be resolved by the two geologists. As the final melting of the European ice sheet accelerated, the Mediterranean Ocean level rose while the Black Sea, as an almost completely empty lake bed, lay 6,000 feet lower in elevation than the Mediterranean Sea. As the sea level in the Mediterranean steadily increased in height, a 6,000-foot wall of water built up against the Bosporus land bridge, less than 30 miles west of the empty Black Sea, until the land bridge began to leak, then after a short time, completely collapse.

Ryan and Pitman estimated that the flow of water rushing through such a narrow passage was probably two hundred times bigger than the total flow down the Niagara Falls. It was the kind of hydraulic power that could easily cut the deep trench in bedrock that the Woods Hole people first observed. The Black Sea began to fill with salt water and before long, water was flowing overland across the area now known as Iraq at a rate of a mile a day. Everybody had to run way from it. It covered large parts of what is now Turkey. The final awareness of what had happened began to appear in publications in the 1990s and it attracted the attention of Robert Ballard of *Titanic* fame. He began to explore the Black Sea with submersibles. He found that the salt water from the Mediterranean had filled up all but 300 feet of the 6,000 feet of depth in the Black Sea. The top layer of fresh water was added long after the flood from the Mediterranean ended. The finding of two kinds of shells was evidence of people starting to live again on the shores after the flood had subsided. The most interesting finding of all was Ballard's locating of former coastlines at 300 feet down, on shelves of land some distance from the present shoreline. Evidence of ancient settlements was visible on these shelves. The real flood victims had lived there. Discoveries like these confirm that biblical truth is one form of truth but not superior to any other kind such as musical, artistic, or natural. Biblical truth may be far more important than any other in terms of human destiny but it is not truer than other truths.

7

Using Biological Research Findings for Human Welfare

The Darwinian theory of evolution provides a paradigm within which all contemporary biological research is carried out.
—Denis Alexander,
Rebuilding the Matrix, 2001

Appendix B at the end of this book lists some of the advances made in biological research and technology in the course of the 20th century. If one looks at this list, one will find that the numbers of advances increase as time passes because every discovery in biology helps other researchers and speeds up the time it takes to make new breakthroughs. Today the rate at which new discoveries are being made in biology is far ahead of the rate for the year 2000. Altogether, three critical discoveries over the past 150 years are responsible for the amazing breakthroughs now being witnessed: The theory of evolution that Darwin presented to the world in 1859 became the great organizing concept within which all biological research has been conducted; about 100 years after that, in 1953, the structure of the DNA molecule was discovered, giving researchers access to the building blocks of life, the genes that define and guide all life forms; then, about 50 years after DNA, in the year 2000, the complete human genome was mapped and the results made available freely to all. The different ways in which these discoveries affect human life are extraordinary and numerous and they touch everyone at some stage of life. In this final chapter, this book will look at some of the ways in which

164

the findings from biological research and the accompanying technologies are improving our lives.

The first successes in joining genes to form a new organism began in California over 30 years ago when scientists combined *E.coli* genes to a monkey virus. The name given to this technology was recombinant DNA. In the early stages it was a very slow process as many of the chemical sequences that make up the DNA had still to be discovered. Furthermore it was difficult to create a genetic code because of the tiny quantities involved. In any cell the amount of chemical substances can be a million times smaller than the amount in a single drop of water. Droplets of nucleotides frequently tended to evaporate before one could add the next ingredient. The ink-jet printer, the familiar attachment to computers that deposits billions of tiny dots of ink in a short time, solved the problem. Cartridges were loaded with nucleotides instead of ink, one cartridge for each of As, Cs, Gs, and Ts. Once the humane genome was available all the preparatory work was done and gene therapy could be tackled from a base of complete human genetic information. For some time, especially in the early days, there was great fear that recombinant DNA would create unpredictable and unmanageable monsters. Conferences were held to examine ways of preventing such outcomes. Over time, these fears were shown to be largely misplaced. A consensus emerged that an altered species does not easily survive in the general environment.

In 2005 the genome of the chimpanzee was completed and warmly hailed by biologists as a huge aid to a better understanding of the human equivalent. Francis Collins, National Genome Research Institute director called it a historic achievement. From it, scientists now know that humans share with chimps more than 96 percent of DNA sequences and this knowledge will greatly help as scientists peer into evolution's lab notebooks. For example, gene therapy is one of the great frontiers of possible medical cures, and the more that is learned of the history of human genes, the better equipped scientists are to modify and use them in such ways as are illustrated in the figure on page 165. One can understand time's influence on genes when one looks back millions of years. In the six million years since humans and chimps diverged from a common ancestor, just to take one example, the typical human protein experienced only one unique change in all of that time. Another vital discovery from the chimp genome

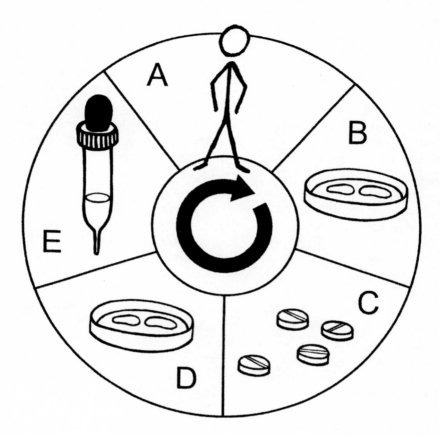

Gene Therapy: A, patient with damaged gene; B, damaged cells extracted; C, cells from a donor with good genes; D, good gene replaces bad one; E, using a virus to carry it, the revised gene is transferred back to the patient.

was the recognition of a gene that helps to protect chimps from Alzheimer's disease. Humans apparently lost that gene! Could it be discovered and used in humans? In spite of the similarities between chimps and humans there are 35 million differences between their DNA sequences. By comparing the two species, researchers hope to find out what DNA changes in humans led to their distinctive characteristics, such features as walking upright, having a greatly enlarged brain, and being able to employ complex forms of language.

Discoveries and Cures

Gene therapy is certainly one of the important branches of research and practice in molecular medicine because a single cure can profoundly change the lives of millions. In earlier days infectious diseases were the scourges of humanity. Improved public health programs in the years following World War II, along with immunization and the use of antibiotics, greatly reduced the numbers affected. Now people are faced with diseases that are different from all of these older ones because they deal with genes, and gene diseases cannot be cured with antibiotics. There are many thousands of these genetically based diseases and every one demands a good deal of research, testing in small animals and then among a number of humans, before it can be declared safe for general use. The number of attempts at cures from gene therapy are many, the successes much fewer. The story of Rhys, an 18-month-old boy from southern Wales, is one of the successful ones. This boy suffered form severe combined immunodeficiency (SCID), a problem caused by a single mutated gene resulting in a condition that required him to live in a sterile environment all the time in order to avoid catching a life-threatening infection. About one in 75,000 births experience this problem. Rhys was known as the bubble boy because of his enforced isolation.

Scientists at Great Ormond Street Hospital in London, England, successfully corrected the imbalance in Rhys' immune system in 2002 and he is now living a normal life. Prior to 2002 the only known treatment was to secure a bone marrow transplant, but for Rhys a matching donor could not be found. The medical team at Great Ormond Street therefore took bone marrow from the boy, then used a virus, just as illustrated in Figure Seven, to carry a new version of the gene into immune cells from the marrow. The marrow was then returned to the boy. Gradually it began to generate new cells. These cells passed into the blood stream and began to protect the boy from infection. Subsequently, other children were successfully cured by the same method, one in London at the same hospital and several others in France. Hemophilia is another, very different kind of genetic disorder. People who have it bleed easily, even from a very small injury, because their blood fails to clot normally. It has been a difficult problem to cure and success to date is only partial. It took eight years of research and experimentation to move from a cure in mice to a cure in dogs. This was achieved by using multiple gene transfer strategies. Finally, in 2005, scientists at Stanford University succeeded in transferring a gene to a small number of patients and this action restored normal blood clotting. More success with more patients is needed before this can be regarded as a general cure.

Genetically Altered Babies

The most sensitive and controversial aspect of gene therapy relates to human reproduction. There is always active opposition to any interference with natural processes no matter how beneficial these interferences might be. When the British Human Fertilization and Embryology Authority gave permission to scientists in September of 2005 to genetically alter a fertilized egg, in order to prevent the transmission of a genetic disease, there was uproar from the pro-life and other movements. In their minds this was an unacceptable step toward the creation of designer babies. Prior to this decision British law prohibited any changes to the genetic structure of a cell after fertilization but this new process, it is claimed by its advocates, does not change the nuclear DNA of cells and does not relate in any way to cloning. The scientists involved say it is equivalent to a surrogate mother either donating an egg or carrying the intended parent's child that was conceived through in vitro fertilization. A closer examination of the ways in which scientists plan to prevent disease transmission will help to understand if the plan is beneficial or not. First, one needs to recognize the size of the problem. There are more than 50 of these inherited diseases in the British population and if they are left to become part of the baby they will cause some permanent damage after birth to one or more of the following organs: brain, heart, liver, muscles, or kidney.

Mitochondrial genes are located outside the nucleus of cells. They are small but they are the collectors of a certain number of inherited diseases. One out of 4,000 children born each year will develop one of these mitochondrial diseases, and evidence of their presence usually become apparent before the child reaches the age of 10. The scientists from Britain's University of Newcastle who received permission to alter fertilized eggs remove the offending genes in the following way. First they secure a healthy egg from another woman and remove its nuclear DNA. This donor egg is first checked to make sure that it has healthy mitochondrial genes. The nuclear DNA from the fertilized egg is then inserted into the donor egg. The result is an embryo with nuclear DNA from the parental egg and sperm and with mitochondrial genes from the donor egg. The colloquial term used to describe the baby that is subsequently born is "baby with two mothers." This procedure for dealing with inherited diseases has only just begun so it will be years before evidences of success are available. It is an approach that can only be carried out within in vitro fertilization clinics because it is essential that there be access to fertilized eggs as soon as possible after the beginning of cell division.

There is one aspect of genetic testing as part of a health check that could seriously influence a person's life for the worse. People need to consider it because it raises ethical issues and also because it represents the risks that might accompany gene therapy quite apart from the medical procedures involved. With the popularity of all the progress in molecular science more and more people want to know if there are inherited diseases that might be passed to succeeding generations and if there are ways of preventing such an outcome. In Canada, for example, there is one private in vitro fertilization clinic that undertakes to test an embryo at a very early stage. If a major disease is detected the embryo is then destroyed. This is how the service works: when the embryo is two or three days old, two cells are extracted and mailed by courier to a test center in Detroit, tested there and a report sent back within a day. It all seems like a good thing to do but in the process important private information about particular people is now in the hands of two agencies and it may be difficult to maintain personal privacy about it. There are always agencies anxious to secure such information. Take, for example, the hypothetical case of a family that discovered it had the high probability of cancer when tested. When, at a later time, an application is made for a family life insurance policy and all medical records have to be provided. The chances of a policy that they can afford are slim.

Within the next decade or two it is entirely possible that a person's genetic past and genetic future will be mapped out at birth. The costs of insurance are only one implication from such information and this is unchanged whether it is private or public. In the case of a public system the costs are spread over a total population rather than being carried by a few. Job prospects are another aspect affected by genetic information. No employer wants to get involved in providing health and retirement benefits for someone who may become permanently ill at an early age. It was the high costs of retirement benefits that created a financial crisis for General Motors in the early years of the 21st century. Insurance costs and occupational prospects are two very important considerations relating to genetic data but they are not the only ones. Take, for example, the case of a person who is strongly disposed to one form of Alzheimer's disease, one that is untreatable. That person has to travel through life with painful information and prospects that could disturb mental balance. Would it be better if such a person had no information about the disease? This is the kind of question that medical practitioners have to face every day: should they or should they not tell a patient all they know about his or her medical problem? Which course would ensure good mental health?

Risk of Avian Flu Pandemic

In 2005 the United Nations General Assembly called for immediate international mobilization against an avian flu that has already transferred into humans and, by early 2005, killed 61 people in Southeast Asia. There are fears that this virus could become a pandemic and be as destructive as the Spanish flu of 1918, a similar bird to human virus and the cause of the deaths of 50 million people worldwide. This new bird to human virus could be worse than the 1918 one because, while there is much greater knowledge on how to cope with it, there is at the same time far greater and more frequent travel around the world. Finding a vaccine for a new type of virus, one that might change as it moves from bird to human, and then have it available in huge quantities at short notice is a huge challenge. An examination of what happened in Central Africa in the past few years illustrates the problem. Within a year, an outbreak of the deadly Ebola virus took the lives of more than 500 people in the Congo. The source of the virus was unknown for some time, then in December of 2005 a team of scientists found the virus in three species of fruit bats in the Congo. These bats are part of the human food chain in the Congo and it seems likely that the transmission from bird to human occurred in this way. It is the concern that a similar bird or bat to human transmission might develop quickly in Asia that has raised concern everywhere, especially since the 1918 virus, though unknown at that time, was a transfer from bird to humans. In 1918 little was known about viruses and almost nothing was available to provide an adequate cure. Almost 80 years later, with concerns mounting that another flu pandemic could hit the world, scientists set about recreating the 1918 virus so that it could be tested out on lab animals to measure its strength.

First they had to find a human body that had died as a result of the 1918 flu. They found one in Alaska. It had been frozen in the Arctic permafrost soon after death so scientists were able to extract samples of lung tissue from it. The overlapping gene sequences were pieced together from this sample to give the full genome sequence and it was at that point that scientists became fairly certain that some ancestor had originally infected birds and the virus had moved from there into humans. The story at that point seemed to be very close to the present threat from Asia. When tested in mice it was found to be extremely virulent, creating 40,000 more particles in a lung than happens with ordinary flu. All the mice that were tested with the 1918 virus died within six days. Samples of the virus are now stored in a secure vault at the Centers for Disease Control and Prevention in Atlanta, Georgia, but fears exist over the risk of it getting into terrorist hands. The United States is not the only country that reconstituted this virus. The director and staff of the United States Federation of American Scientists' Working Group on Biological Weapons are far from being satisfied with the level of security presently provided in Atlanta. They say that the risk of theft by a disgruntled, disturbed, or extremist lab employee at the facility is so great that it comes close to being inevitable. They have proposed raising the level of security to the highest possible. In 2003, they point out, a SARS virus escaped accidentally from a lab in Singapore and a year later there were two escapes of the same virus from labs in Beijing.

The present avian flu virus has been found in thousands of birds in Asia and in smaller numbers in many other countries, presumably carried worldwide by migrating birds. The detailed gene sequences of this virus are well known. The virus is called H5N1 and it is one that has never before been experienced by humans except for those who died from it in Asia. There are therefore no antibodies in humans that could fight off infections from this virus, as is the case year by year when more familiar strains of flu viruses appear. Dr. Andrew Fauci of the United States National Institute of Health, the United States watchdog for tracing the behavior of the H5N1 virus, monitors it regularly as samples are collected from time to time, to check any mutations that develop and to give warning if any evidence of transfers from human to human are found. At the end of 2005, this had not yet happened. Soon after the first human death from H5N1, Fauci's lab developed a vaccine that would be able to protect humans. It had to be tested out on mice before it was safe to be administered to humans. Fauci discovered that the dosage needed to protect test animals was far greater than required for traditional flu attacks. Thus the various difficulties associated with responding to the United Nations appeal remain: how to produce enough vaccines in a very short time, that is to say once the right mutation is present for creating a pandemic, how to cope with breakdowns in social organizations and institutions if large numbers of people die, and how to equip and protect adequately the care givers in hospitals so that the damage can be minimized.

Designs from Nature for Engineers

Alongside the many scientists who work in gene therapy for preventive and corrective medical cures there is a new group of synthetic biologists bringing to biotechnology the same engineering strategies used to build computers, bridges and buildings. They separate cells into their fundamental components and then rebuild new organisms. It's a complex form of genetic engineering that challenges the notion of what's natural and what's synthetic. In the 19th century chemists learned to synthesize organic compounds to make such new things as plastics and polyesters. The dreams of synthetic biologists go far beyond these achievements. They envisage a new industrial revolution in which plants rely on the biological processing of cells rather than petroleum. Some enterprises have already begun creating products in this way. The Dupont Company that led the field in creating synthetic garments of all kinds in earlier days invested 100 million dollars in a factory in Tennessee in 2005. It will mass produce a new spandex-like fiber based on the raw material of redesigned *E.coli* bacteria. Craig Venter, the leader of the team that mapped a private version of the human genome, received a multi-million dollar grant from the United States Department of Energy to design a clean energy source from the genes of microbes. He hopes to string different genes together to create organisms that can produce alternative fuels such as hydrogen or ethanol.

At the Manchester Center for Nanotechnology in Britain, scientists discovered the secret of the gecko's climbing ability. This lizard, found in warm climates, is able to walk easily on vertical surfaces because of its adhesive feet. Adhesives based on an understanding of the geckos are now being manufactured at the Manchester Center. They will be self-cleaning, dry, and re-attachable, and rock climbers and window washers will use them. These new adhesives contain billions of tiny plastic fibers similar to the hairs that cover the soles of geckos. The discovery in Manchester as well as the ones in which Dupont and Craig Venter are involved are only three of the numerous findings that appeared in recent years as more and more researchers become captivated by the prospects of synthetic biology. There are others that point to revolutions in medical, military, and commercial applications. The jewel beetle lays its eggs in freshly burned trees and, as a result, it can detect fires from miles away. The United States defense industry is studying these beetles for clues that might help them design infrared detectors. NASA learned that abalone shells are extremely strong so it is examining them to see if their genes might provide the kind of coatings required on their impact-resistant thermal tiles. The Swedish car company Volvo has undertaken a study of the behavior of locusts. It had been working on a possible anti-collision device for cars when scientists came up with the finding that these insects swarm in very large numbers yet never strike one another. Volvo wants to know if they have a genetic secret that might contribute to the anti-collision design.

In Canada, unique anti-freeze proteins have been discovered in tiny snow fleas and these are being examined for possible use in the development of frost-resistant plants. These proteins lower the flea's temperature by 10 degrees Fahrenheit. They are also being considered for use in transplanting human organs when demands occur for their preservation at low temperatures during transportation. Scientists from Queen's University, Kingston, collected 100,000 of these fleas from snow banks for their investigations.

Another discovery relates to the hardware employed in hip replacements. In order to give as long a life as possible to these operations, surgeons attach a hard substance to the metal component to ease the pressure from the metal. Over the usual 15 years of maximum life in these operations, this hard substance tends to get brittle and disintegrate. Now there is a new and much tougher material available that will significantly extend the life of hip replacements. It was identified in the teeth of horses and after being separated into its components it was reconstructed and manufactured in quantity. If you look at horses' teeth you will notice that they are brown in color. This is not due to lack of toothpaste and toothbrushes but rather is the result of a very strong coating called cementum. It is this coating that gives horses' teeth their well-known great strength and it is this same reconstituted coating that can and does now extend the life of hip replacements.

The dangers implicit in all forms of synthetic biology are known worldwide. The world's most poisonous gases can be produced by this technique. Undoubtedly terrorists are already working on that aspect of it. Many controls are in place to prevent such usage but the danger remains because almost anyone, with the simplest of lab resources, can create new life forms. One commercial company provides an online genome sequence repository with 40 billion bits of code from different species, as of December 2005. By February of 2006 that amount will have risen to 80 billion bits. One no longer has to be a genetics professor to work at synthetic biology. A computer and access to the Internet is all that is needed and already the attraction of this field is drawing more and more people into it, including many of high school age. The Blue Heron is typical of the types of private enterprises now springing up to service the demand for gene sequences. Its director formerly worked on the human genome project. A researcher can type up and send to Blue Heron by e-mail the genetic code he or she wants to translate into an organism. The e-mail is automatically transformed into chemical dots by a machine specially designed for this purpose, synthesized, and sent back within 24 hours inside bacteria as the carrier. Blue Heron charged about 16 dollars for a DNA base pair in 2001. Four years later, in response to much higher volume, the price was less than two dollars.

Conclusion

This book is about the importance of modern science and the tragedy of fundamentalist rejection of it, particularly the rejection of the theory of evolution, that essential part of modern science. Almost all medical discoveries and breakthroughs depend on it. Despite its vital role, for more than a hundred years creationists—now better known as intelligent designers or IDs—have maintained an endless attack on it. This book traced the history of this movement from its inception in the early decades of the 19th century right up to the present time. Throughout that period of time, people have seen the emergence of all kinds of so-called scientific alternatives to evolution: creationism, creation science, flood theology, and now intelligent design. Sadly, as this book demonstrated in Chapter 2, these fundamentalists—evangelical Christians for the most part—in recent times decided to engage in political activism to secure their ends. Thoughtful people accused them of trying to change America from a democracy into a theocracy. In that connection, here is a quote on a similar situation from the former moderator of the Dutch Reformed Church of South Africa, in relation to his church's support of Apartheid, "We never again want political power. We made such a mess of it when we had it."

Fundamentalists insist that they are not opposed to science. They say they welcome it but what they welcome is the old form of science, common sense science, the one that introduced the modern phase of science in the 17th century. Its origins lay in the work of Francis Bacon and it was developed and introduced to America through the work of Thomas Reid of Aberdeen University in Scotland. It fitted perfectly into traditional interpretations of the Bible because its hallmark was the right and the ability of every individual to interpret the Bible for himself or herself. At the time of the American Revolution with Jefferson's insistence on inalienable human rights and democracy, it was easy for the evangelical Christians of that time to make common cause with the nation's political leaders. The science of common sense gave convincing support to traditional interpretations of the Bible, particularly its literal infallibility. Restoration movements sprang up from time to time, attempting to recreate the conditions of 1776, seen by them as the golden age of American life.

The zenith of fundamentalist opposition to evolution came in the early years of the 20th century. Evangelicals arranged a series of 12 publications, written by theologians from different countries. They had them appropriately titled *The Fundamentals*. Appendix A at the end of this book lists the contents of each of these books. They were intended to be definitive statements of the beliefs of evangelical Christians and it was soon evident from their content that the rejection of evolution was central to all that was written. Closely allied to the rejection of evolution was the rejection of all forms of modern literary criticism. Many hundreds of thousands of these books were distributed to evangelical leaders throughout the world. The hope of the authors was that these books would unite all evangelicals in a crusade against science. The result was the opposite. Over the first three decades of the 20th century, two camps of evangelical Christians emerged: a majority of fundamentalists and a minority of the rest. The central reality that united fundamentalists then, and still does today, was and is their belief in the literal infallibility of the Bible. What they seldom recognized was that their position was a matter of interpretation, not of the truth or error of the Bible, and for this reason Chapter 6 of this book is devoted to the subject of biblical interpretation.

It is difficult to see how evangelical fundamentalism can be changed after all of these years, yet within the latter part of 2005 and in the year 2006 several gains can be seen. In the middle of 2005 it seemed that one school board in Pennsylvania, the Dover School Board, was about to succeed in imposing intelligent design as a science equal to evolution in its public schools. A few parents launched a court challenge to what was about to take place and the case was argued out in the District Court in Harrisburg. Many schools across the country anxiously watched the proceedings, wondering if similar curricula would be imposed on their schools if Dover won its case. Michael Behe, one of the outstanding leaders of the intelligent design movement, was defending the decision of the school board. Behe had been honored by the evangelical Christian community through its journal *Christianity Today* when his book, *Darwin's Black Box*, was given the book of the year award. The Harrisburg decision rejected outright the Dover School Board's plan and extracts from its findings are listed in Appendix C. They show clearly the major contradictions and errors in Behe's presentations.

In 2006, books that oppose the central theme of the intelligent design movement are beginning to appear. That central theme is the idea of irreducible complexity. One book by Francis Collins, an evangelical Christian and the person who was head of the NIH human genome project, points out in his latest book, *The Language of God*, that the idea of irreducible complexity is no longer tenable. Researchers in molecular biology see it as an old-fashioned concept, once useful at the time when the unknowns of science were resolved by a god-of-the-gaps philosophy. Evangelical fundamentalists have been able to demonize the theory of evolution. Fewer and fewer young people are taking science degrees. The United States is 25th among developed countries, with less than six percent of its college graduates taking science degrees. Federal money for scientific research, per capita, is far below many other countries, yet it is the wealthiest nation on earth. Presently the government of Singapore leads the world in per capita financial support of biological research, particularly stem cell research. Developments such as these new books and the rejection of the Dover School Board's attempts to equate the pseudo-science of intelligent design with the theory of evolution are all helpful, but the United States has a long way to go if it is going to restore its international standing in science.

APPENDIX A

Preface and Tables of Contents for The Fundamentals: A Testimony to the Truth

Volumes One to Twelve

Compliments of
Two Christian Laymen

Testimony Publishing Company
(Not Inc.)
808 North La Salle Street
Chicago, Ill., U.S.A.

A Statement by the Two Laymen

Rev. A.C. Dixon, D.D., in the fall of 1909, while pastor of the Moody Church in Chicago, organized the Testimony Publishing Company. He also edited the first five volumes of "The Fundamentals," but upon being called to London early in the summer of 1911 to become pastor of the Metropolitan Tabernacle, founded by the late Charles H. Spurgeon, he found it necessary to give up the editorial work on the books.

The next five books were taken in hand by the late Louis Meyer, a Christian Jew, who worked so strenuously in the securing and editing of matter for "The Fundamentals" that his health failed. He departed to be with Christ July 11, 1913, in Monrovia, California. His widow and children are new residing in Pasadena, California.

Rev. R.A. Torrey, D.D., Dean of the Bible Institute of Los Angeles, edited Volumes XI and XII, two articles, however, in Volume XI having been approved by Dr. Meyer and passed on to Dr. Torrey when he took up the work.

179

The following are the names of the original Committee to whom was committed full supervision of the movement: Rev. A.C. Dixon, D.D., Rev. R.A. Torrey, D.D., Rev. Louis Meyer, D.D. (deceased 1913), Mr. Henry P. Crowell, Mr. Thomas S. Smith, Mr. D.W. Potter, Rev. Elmore Harris, D.D. (deceased 1911).

The following names were added later to the foregoing: Prof. Joseph Kyle, D.D., LL.D., Prof. Charles R. Erdman, D.D., Mr. Delavan L. Pierson, Rev. L.W. Munhall, D.D., Rev. T.C. Horton, Rev. H.C. Mabie, D.D., Rev. John Balcom Shaw, D.D.

To these men for their always efficient and painstaking service, rendered practically without any material remuneration whatever, are due the heartfelt thanks, not only of the Two Laymen, but of the thousand who have received the books. Every member of the Committee, without exception, has been faithful to his trust.

Mr. Giles Kellogg has been the Los Angeles trustee of the Testimony funds, and Mr. J.S. McGlashan the Chicago trustee. The Walton and Spencer Company of Chicago have been the printers. The faithful services rendered by all of these thoroughly merit this word of appreciation.

Mr. Thomas E. Stephens, editor of the "Moody Church Herald," has been the Business Manager from the beginning, and the Moody Church and Moody Bible Institute have contributed in many ways to the success of the work.

The original plan was for twelve volumes to be issued, one every two or three months, but owing to the difficulty of realizing on securities that had been put up for this work, the intervals between the later volumes have been greatly prolonged, but with the present volume, the original plan is complete.

It may be of interest to state that over 2,500,000 copies of the twelve volumes have been published and circulated, and that the call for back volumes has been so insistent as to make necessary the reprinting of over a quarter of a million additional copies of the earlier issues, this bringing the total output up to nearly 3,000,000 copies.

Approximately one-third of these 3,000,000 copies have gone to countries outside of the United States. About one-half of the latter have been sent to various parts of Great Britain, and the rest to other foreign countries. The great majority of Protestant missionary workers of the world have received them. The present mailing list comprises about 100,000 addresses of Christian workers, all of whom have asked for "The Fundamentals."

Since the movement began, some 200,000 letters have been received, including many requests for the continuance of this testimony in some form. In compliance with these requests, it is planned to undertake its continuous through "The King's Business,," which is published by the Bible Institute of Los Angeles, and of which Dr. Torrey will be the editor-in-chief. Dr. Torrey was for many years the Superintendent of the Moody Bible Institute of Chicago, until he left that work to undertake his world-wide work as an evangelist. He is now Dean of the Bible Institute of Los Angeles.

The Testimony Publishing Company, from the very inception of its work of publishing "The Fundamentals," has been absolutely free of commercialism. Any profits arising from subscriptions to the magazine are to be used for free Scripture and tract distribution and missionary work.

It is purposed for "The King's Business" not merely to give the best articles that can be secured along the line of testimony of the twelve volumes of "The Fundamentals," but also to make helps on the International Sunday School lessons a special feature of the magazine. We assume that in doing this, a need will be supplied which will greatly increase the effectiveness of Sunday School teaching. In conclusion, we would state that arrangements have been made to send the April number of "The King's Business" to all the readers of "The Fundamentals."

Volume One Contents

Volume Two Contents

Volume Three Contents

Volume Four Contents

Volume Five Contents

Volume Six Contents

Volume Seven Contents

Volume Eight Contents

Volume Nine Contents

Volume Ten Contents

Volume Eleven Contents

Volume Twelve Contents

APPENDIX B

Medical Breakthroughs
Over 100 Years

1905 to 1930

1905 Aspirin in general use
1905 Hormones identified
1906 Eye cornea transplants
1922 Insulin discovered
1928 Typhus controlled through improvements in hygiene
1928 Penicillin
1929 Chemotherapy for cancer

1930 to 1955

1932 Electron microscope
1939 Plastic surgery
1943 Kidney dialysis
1944 Open heart surgery
1948 Cortisone in use
1949 Tranquilizers
1950 Kidney transplants
1953 DNA double helix discovered
1953 Polio vaccine
1955 Birth control pill

1955 to 1980

1957 Ultrasound technology in use
1958 Artificial pacemaker developed
1959 Linking severe loss of dopamine with Parkinson's
1960 Repair of congenital dislocation of the hip
1964 Laser surgery
1965 Endoscope developed
1967 Cat scans

1967 Heart transplant
1968 Bone marrow transplant
1969 Artificial heart
1977 Smallpox eradicated
1977 Magnetic resonance imaging
1978 In vitro fertilization

1980 to 2005

1982 Prion (mad cow disease) identified
1989 Cystic fibrosis gene identified
1990 Beginnings of gene therapy
1994 Fetal surgery
1995 High flux beam reactor for reducing pain in bone cancer
1997 Cloning
1997 Growing new body organs from cells
1997 Triggering growth of new blood vessels in wounds
1998 Bone reconstruction using a biodegradable foam
1999 Identifying genes involved in human body movements
1999 Diphtheria toxins analyzed
2000 Human genome completed
2002 Bubble Boy syndrome (SCID) cured by gene therapy
2002   Non-surgical cure for cataracts developed
2005 New treatment for diabetes
2005 Diagnosis of role of multiple genes in schizophrenia

APPENDIX C

Extracts from the Judgment of United States District Court, Harrisburg, Pennsylvania, December 20, 2005, Regarding the Dover Area School District

ID?

After a searching review of the record and applicable case law, we find that while ID arguments may be true, a proposition on which the Court takes no position, ID is not science. We find that ID fails on three different levels, any one of which is sufficient to preclude a determination that ID is science. They are: (1) ID violates the centuries-old ground rules of science by invoking and permitting supernatural causation; (2) the argument of irreducible complexity, central to ID, employs the same flawed and illogical contrived dualism that doomed creation science in the 1980s; and (3) ID's negative attacks on evolution have been refuted by the scientific community. It is additionally important to note that ID has failed to gain acceptance in the scientific community, it has not generated peer-reviewed publications, nor has it been the subject of testing and research.

Expert testimony reveals that since the scientific revolution of the 16th and 17th centuries, science has been limited to the search for natural causes to explain natural phenomena. This revolution entailed the rejection of the appeal to authority, and by extension, revelation, in favor of empirical evidence. Since that time period, science has been a discipline in which testability, rather than any ecclesiastical authority or philosophical coherence, has been the measure of a scientific idea's worth. In deliberately omitting theological or "ultimate" explanations for the existence or characteristics of the natural world, science does not consider issues of "meaning" and "purpose" in the world. While supernatural explanations may be important and have merit, they are not part of science. This self-imposed convention of science, which limits inquiry to testable, natural explanations about the natural world, is referred to by philosophers as "methodological naturalism" and is sometimes known as the scientific method. Methodological naturalism is a "ground rule" of science today and it requires scientists to seek explanations in the world around us based upon what we can observe, test, replicate, and verify.

As the National Academy of Sciences (NAS) was recognized by experts for both parties in this case as the "most prestigious" scientific association in this country, we will accordingly cite its opinion where appropriate. NAS is in agreement that the science is limited to empirical, observable and ultimately testable data: "Science is a particular way of knowing about the world. In science, explanations are restricted to those that can be inferred from the confirmable data—the results obtained through observations and experiments that can be substantiated by other scientists. Anything that can be observed or measured is amenable to scientific investigation. Explanations that cannot be based upon empirical evidence are not part of science."

This rigorous attachment to "natural" explanations is an essential attribute to science by definition and by convention. From a practical perspective, attributing unsolved problems about nature to causes and forces that lie outside the natural world is a "science stopper." Once you attribute a cause to an untestable supernatural force, a proposition that cannot be disproven, there is no reason to continue seeking natural explanations as we have our answer. ID is predicated on supernatural causation, as we previously explained and as various expert testimony revealed. ID takes a natural phenomenon and, instead of accepting or seeking a natural explanation, argues that the explanation is supernatural. Further support for the conclusion that ID is predicated on supernatural causation is found in the ID reference book to which ninth grade biology students are directed, *Pandas*. Stated another way, ID posits that animals did not evolve naturally through evolutionary means but were created abruptly by a non-natural, or supernatural, designer.

ID aspires to "change the ground rules" of science and lead defense expert Professor Behe admitted that his broadened definition of science, which encompasses ID, would also embrace astrology. Moreover, defense expert Professor Minnich acknowledged that for ID to be considered science, the ground rules of science have to be broadened to allow consideration of supernatural forces. Prominent ID leaders are in agreement with the opinions expressed by defense expert witnesses that the ground rules of science must be changed for ID to take hold and prosper. William Dembski, for instance, an ID leader, proclaims that science is ruled by methodological naturalism and argues that this rule must be overturned if ID is to prosper. Indeed, entire fields of inquiry, including especially in the human sciences, will need to be rethought from the ground up in terms of intelligent design. The Discovery Institute, the think tank promoting ID acknowledges in its Wedge Document as "Governing Goals" to defeat scientific materialism and its destructive moral, cultural and political legacies and replace materialistic explanations with the theistic understanding that nature and human beings are created by God.

This Wedge Document states in its "Five Year Strategic Plan Summary" that the IDM's goal is to replace science as currently practiced with "theistic and Christian science." Accordingly it seeks nothing less than a complete scientific revolution in which ID will supplant evolutionary theory. The Wedge Strategy is composed of three phases: Phase I is scientific research, writing and publicity; Phase II is publicity and opinion-making; and Phase III is cultural confrontation and renewal. In the "Five Year Strategic Plan Summary," the Wedge Document explains that the social consequences of materialism have been "devastating" and that it is necessary to broaden the wedge with a positive scientific alternative to materialistic scientific theories, namely the theory of ID.

Notably, every major scientific association that has taken a position on the issue of whether ID is science has concluded that ID is not, and cannot be considered as such. Initially, we note that NAS, the "most prestigious" scientific association in the country, views ID as follows: Creationism, intelligent design, and other claims of supernatural intervention in the origin of life or of species are not science because they are not testable by the methods of science. These claims subordinate observed data to statements based on authority, revelation, or religious belief. Documentation offered in support of these claims is typically limited to the special publications of their advocates. These publications do not offer hypotheses subject to change in light of new data, new interpretations, or demonstration of error. This contrasts with science, where any hypothesis or theory always remains subject to the possibility of rejection or modification in the light of new knowledge.

The American Association for the Advancement of Science (AAAS), the largest organization of scientists in this country, has taken a similar position on ID, namely, that it "has not proposed a scientific means of testing its claims" and that the lack of scientific warrant for so-called 'intelligent design theory' makes it improper to include as part of science education. Not a single expert witness over the course over the course of the six week trial identified one major scientific association, society or organization that endorsed ID as science. What is more, defense experts concede that ID is not a theory as that term is defined by the NAS and admit that ID is at best "fringe science" which has achieved no acceptance in the scientific community.

It is therefore readily apparent to the Court that ID fails to meet the essential ground rules that limit science to testable, natural explanations. Science cannot be defined differently for Dover students that it is defined in the scientific community. ID is at bottom premised upon a false dichotomy, namely, that to the extent evolutionary theory is discredited, ID is confirmed. This argument is not brought to this Court anew since the same argument, termed "contrived dualism," was employed by creationists in the 1980's to support "creation science." At that time the court noted the "fallacious pedagogy of the two model approach," that all evidence which criticized evolutionary theory was proof in support of creation science. We do not find this false dichotomy any more availing to justify ID today than it was to justify creation science two decades ago.

We note that irreducible complexity as defined by Professor Behe in his book *Darwin's Black Box* and subsequently modified in his 2001 article entitled "Reply to My Critics," appears as follows: by irreducibly complex I mean a single system which is composed of several well-matched, interacting parts that contribute to the basic function, wherein the removal of any one of the parts causes the system to effectively cease functioning. An irreducibly complex system cannot be produced directly by slight, successive modifications of a precursor system, because any precursor to an irreducibly complex system that is missing a part is by definition non-functional ... Since natural selection can only choose systems that are already working, then if a biological system cannot be produced gradually it would have to arise as an integrated unit, in one fell swoop, for natural selection to have anything to act on. Professor Behe admitted in "Reply to my Critics" that there was a defect in his view of irreducible complexity because, while it purports to be a challenge to natural selection, it does not actually address "the task facing natural selection." Professor Behe wrote that he hoped to "repair this defect in future work;" however, he has failed to do so even four years after elucidating his defect.

The conclusion that the design seen in life is real design is a restatement of the Reverend William Paley's argument applied at the cell level, except that Professor Behe refuses to identify the designer, whereas Paley inferred from the presence of design that it was God. The design of biological systems is based upon an analogy to human design. Because we are able to recognize design of artifacts and objects, according to Professor Behe, that same reasoning can be employed to determine biological design. Professor Behe testified that the strength of the analogy depends upon the degree of similarity entailed in the two propositions; however, if this is the test, ID completely fails. Unlike biological systems, human artifacts do not live and reproduce over time. They are non-replicable, they do not undergo genetic recombination, and they are not driven by natural selection. For human artifacts, we know the designer's identity, human, and the mechanism of design, as we have experience based upon empirical evidence that humans can make such things, as well as many other attributes including the designer's abilities, needs, and desires.

With ID, proponents assert that they refuse to propose hypotheses on the designer's identity, do not propose a mechanism, and the designer, he/she/it/they, has never been seen. In that vein, defense expert Professor Minnich agreed that in the case of human artifacts and objects, we know the identity and capacities of the human designer, but we do not know any of those attributes for the designer of biological life. In addition, Professor Behe agreed that for the design of human artifacts, we know the designer and its attributes and we have a baseline for human design that does not exist for design of biological systems. Professor Behe's only response to these seemingly insurmountable points of disanalogy was that the inference still works in science fiction movies. It is readily apparent to the Court that the only attribute of design that biological systems appear to share with human artifacts is their complex appearance, i.e. if it looks complex or designed, it must have been designed.

ID proponents generally and *Pandas* specifically, distort and misrepresent scientific knowledge in making their anti-evolution argument. This book to which students are expressly referred presents *Pandas* as representative of ID. A series of arguments against evolutionary theory found in it which studies the life of the past and the fossil record. First, it misrepresents the "dominant form of understanding relationships" between organisms, namely, the tree of life, represented by classification determined via the method of cladistics. Second, *Pandas* misrepresents "homology," the "central concept of comparative biology," that allowed scientists to evaluate comparable parts among organisms for classification purposes for hundreds of years. Third, *Pandas* fails to address the well-established biological concept of exaptation, which involves a structure changing function, such as fish fins evolving fingers and bones to become legs for weight-bearing land animals.

Pandas presents discredited science. Its treatment of biochemical similarities between organisms is "inaccurate and downright false," *Pandas* misrepresents basic molecular biology concepts and misinforms readers on the standard evolutionary relationships between different types of animals, a distortion which Professor Behe affirmed. In addition *Pandas'* claim that evolution cannot account for new genetic information is referred by more than three dozen peer-reviewed scientific publications showing the origin of new genetic information by evolutionary processes. In summary *Pandas* misrepresents molecular biology and genetic principles, as well as the current state of scientific knowledge in those areas, in order to teach readers that common decent and natural selection are not scientifically sound. Accordingly, the one textbook to which the Dover ID Policy directs students contains outdated concepts and badly flawed science.

After this searching and careful review of ID as espoused by its proponents, as elaborated upon in submissions to the Court, and as scrutinized over a six week trial, we find that ID is not science and cannot be adjudged a valid, accepted scientific theory. ID, as noted, is grounded in theology, not science. ID's backers have sought to avoid the scientific scrutiny which we have now determined it cannot withstand by advocating that the *controversy*, but not ID itself, should be taught in science class. This tactic is at best disingenuous, and at worst a canard. The goal of ID is not to encourage critical thought, but to foment a revolution which would supplant evolutionary theory with ID. To conclude and reiterate, we express no opinion on the ultimate veracity of ID as a supernatural explanation. However, we commend to the attention of those who are inclined to consider ID to be a true "scientific" alternative to evolution the foregoing detailed analysis. It is our view that a reasonable, objective observer would, after reviewing both the voluminous record and our narrative, reach the inescapable conclusion that ID is an interesting theological argument, but that it is not science.

Glossary

Adaptation: features of organisms that aid survival and reproduction.

Allele: a gene that occupies a particular place on a chromosome.

Amino acid: the basic building block of a protein. In the average living organism, there are as many as 20 of these amino acids.

Baconian science: the earliest form of modern science, common in the 18th century. The name comes from Sir Francis Bacon, a British scientist.

Bacteria: micro organisms that show an enormous range of abilities, and are able to live in extremes of temperature and other difficult environmental conditions.

Biological determinism: the claim that the characteristics of organisms are due to their genes only and therefore not subject to environment.

Burgess Shale: a sedimentary unit forming part of a formation in the Rocky Mountains of British Columbia. This formation is over 500 million years old and is known worldwide for its enormous quantity of fossils.

Catastrophism: a belief that earth's history is dominated by major upheavals.

Chromosome: threadlike links that carry the genes within the center of a cell.

Cladistics: the science of identifying characteristics that determine whether species are distantly or closely related.

Common sense science: the earliest form of modern science, common in the eighteenth century. See Baconian science. The name, common sense, comes from the work of Thomas Reid, a Scottish scientist.

Contingency: a more technical term for the word chance and it is the notion that unexpected events occur.

Creation science: a system claiming that scientific evidence supports the story of creation in the early part of the book of Genesis.

Darwinism: a term usually applied to Darwin's statement that natural selection is the main causal factor in evolution.

Day-age creationism: a view that relates to scientific findings by interpreting each of the six days of creation as very long periods of time.

Deism: a belief that God works only through fixed laws without using miracles.

Disparity: the variety of different types of animal fossils found at any one period of time, each type of animal having the same basic anatomy and morphology.

Diversity: the total number of species or higher levels of organisms at a given point of time.

DNA: the molecule that transmits genetic information.

Empiricism: the view that knowledge must be based on experience through the five senses.

Evolutionary creationism: the view that God the creator uses the method of evolution to form the universe.

Gap creationists: people who say there is a huge time gap between Genesis 1:1 and Genesis 1: 2 and this gap explains the apparent great age of the earth.

Gene therapy: altering the genetic structure of an organism, especially in humans, to eliminate genetic diseases.

Genetic drift: accidents of mating in small populations that can outweigh the effects of natural selection.

Genome: the totality of DNA in an organism.

Geocentrists: those who deny that the sun is the center of the solar system. This was the commonly-held view 400 years ago.

Geological time: time normally measured by radiometric methods, that is to say the measurement of the decay of radioactive substances which is a constant and enables scientists to tell how old a particular rock is.

Hominids: forms of life anatomically similar to humans, able to walk on two legs.

Inductive bible study: observing, interpreting, and applying practically the meanings of Bible verses without the use of philosophical, theological or experiential guidelines.

Intelligent design creationists: a modern form of Natural Theology, that is the view that the work of a creator is evident in his creation.

Morphology: the study of organic form.

Natural Selection: Darwin's proposed mechanism for evolutionary change, namely that a small percentage of organisms in each generation survive and reproduce because they possess characteristics which other members of the same group do not possess. Now regarded as one possible mechanism.

Natural theology: The long standing view that something of the nature of the creator can be seen in his creation.

Neanderthals: pre-human hominids.

Old—earth creationists: People who accept the great age of the earth but insist that God was and is personally involved as an active agent.

Palaeontologist: a person who studies fossils.

Plankton: organisms that float in the water column.

Recombinant DNA: The joining of genes from two or more organisms to form a new organism. This process is sometimes called synthetic biology.

Speciation: the formation of new species.

Species: the basic unit of biology, defined on the basis of the group's ability to interbreed and produce fertile offspring.

Synthetic biology: see recombinant DNA.

Theism: the belief that God intervenes in his creation.

Trace fossil: the remains of the activity of an organism. Maybe a hole or a burrow left by a worm or a trail left by a sea creature.

Trilobites: a now extinct animal that flourished prior to 250 million years ago.

Uniformitarianism: the claim that events in the geological past can be explained in terms of those operating today.

Young-earth creationists: those who reject modern views of the age of the earth and insist that it is only thousands rather than billions of years old.

Zygote: the union of a male and female cell at an early stage of human reproduction.

Bibliography

Aldridge, Bill G. (Ed.). (1996). *Scope, Sequence, and Coordination: A High School Framework for Science Education.* Arlington, VA: National Science Teachers Association (NSTA).

Alexander, Denis. (2001). *Rebuilding the Matrix: Science and Faith in the Twenty-first Century.* Grand Rapids: Zondervan.

Asimov, Isaac. (1981). *In the Beginning.* New York: Crown Publishers Inc.

Bebbington, David. (1989). *Evangelicalism in Modern Britain: A History from the 1730s to the 1980s.* London: Unwin Hyman/Routledge.

Behe, Michael J. (1996). *Darwin's Black Box: The Biochemical Challenge to Evolution.* New York: Free Press.

Boorstin, Daniel J. (1985). *The Discoverers: A History of Man's Search to Know His World and Himself.* New York: Random House.

Crane, Nicholas. (2002). *Mercator: The Man who Mapped the Planet.* London: Weidenfeld and Nicholson.

Cuvier, Georges. (1817). *Essay on the Theory of the Earth.* Edinburgh: William Blackwood.

Danielson, Dennis R. (2000). *The Book of the Cosmos: Imagining the Universe from Heraclitus to Hawking.* Cambridge, Mass: Perseus Publishing.

Darwin, Charles R. (1859). *On the Origin of Species by Means of Natural Selection.* London: John Murray.

Dawkins, Richard. (1976). *The Selfish Gene.* New York: Oxford University Press.

De Hamel, Christopher. (2001). *The Book: A History of the Bible.* London: Phaidon Press Limited

Dembski, William A., and Kushiner, James M. (2001) *Signs of Intelligence.* Grand Rapids: Brazos Press.

Department of Divinity. (1995). *But Where Shall Wisdom Be Found?* Initium Sapientiae Timor Domini. Aberdeen: Aberdeen University Press.

Devine, T. M. (1999). *The Scottish Nation: 1700-2000.* London: The Penguin Group.

Edwards, David L. and Stott, John. (1988). *Essentials: A Liberal-Evangelical Dialogue.* London: Hodder and Stoughton.

Gould, Stephen Jay. (1999). *Rocks of Ages: Science and Religion in the Fullness of Life.* New York: Random House Inc.

Gould, Stephen J. (2002). *The Structure of Evolutionary Theory.* Cambridge: Harvard University Press.

Herman, Arthur. (2001). *How the Scots Invented the Modern World.* London: Open Court Publishing Company.

Huggett, Richard. (1989). *Cataclysms and Earth History.* Oxford: 1989

201

Hutton, James. (1795). *Theory of the Earth with Proofs and Illustrations, 2 vols*. Edinburgh: William Creech.

Johnson, Paul. (1983). *Modern Times: The World from the Twenties to the Eighties*. New York: Harper and Row.

Johnson, Phillip E and Lamoureux, Denis O. (1999). *Darwinism Defeated?* Vancouver: Regent College Publishing.

La Follette, Marclel C. (Ed). *Creationism, Science, and the Law: The Arkansas Case*. Cambridge, Mass: MIT Press.

Larson, Edward J. (2003, 3rd ed). *Trial and Error: The American Controversy Over Creation and Evolution*. New York: Oxford University Press.

Lerner, Lawrence S. (2000). *Good Science, Bad Science: Teaching Evolution in the States*. Washington, D.C.: Thomas B. Fordham Foundation.

Marsden, George M. (1980). *Fundamentalism and American Culture*. New York: Oxford University Press.

Malthus, Thomas. (1798). *An Essay on the Principle of Population as It Affects the Future Improvement of Society*. London: J. Johnson.

Morris, Henry M. (1961). *The Genesis Flood: The Biblical Record and its Scientific Implications*. Philadelphia: Presbyterian and Reformed Publishing Company.

Morris, Henry M., and Parker, Gary E. (1982). *What is Creation Science?* El Cajon: Creation-Life Publishers.

Morris, Conway C. (1998). *The Crucible of Creation: The Burgess Shale and the Rise of Animals*. New York: Oxford University Press.

Morris, Conway, C. (2003). *Life's Solutions: Inevitable Humans in a Lonely Universe*. Cambridge: Cambridge University Press.

National Research Council. (1996). *The National Science Education Standards*. Washington, DC: National Academy Press.

Numbers, Ronald L. (1992). *The Creationists*. New York: Alfred A. Knopf.

Packer, J I. (1958). *Fundamentalism and the Word of God*. London: Inter-Varsity Press.

Paley, William. (1963 edited by Frederick Ferre). *Natural Theology*. Indianapolis: Bobbs-Merrill Company.

Polanyi, Michael. (1958). *Personal Knowledge*. London: Routledge and Kegan Paul.

Polkinghorne, John. (1998). *Belief in God in an Age of Science*. New Haven: Yale University Press.

Reid, Thomas. (1997 edited by Derek R Brookes). *An Inquiry into the Human Mind on the Principles of Common Sense*. University Park: Pennsylvania State University Press.

Ruse, Michael. (2003). *Darwin and Design*. Cambridge: Harvard University Press.

Ryan, William and Pitman, Walter. (1998). *Noah's Flood: the New Scientific Discoveries about the Event that Changed History*. New York: Simon and Schuster.

Sandeen, Ernest R. (1970). *The Roots of Fundamentalism*. Chicago: University of Chicago Press.

Santillana, Georgio de. (1955). *The Crime of Galileo*. Chicago: University of Chicago Press.

Singer, Charles. (1959). *A Short History of Scientific Ideas to 1900*. Oxford: The Clarendon Press.

Stewart, John. (2000). *Evolution's Arrow: The Direction of Evolution and the Future of Humanity*. Canberra, Australia: Chapman Press.

Towne, Margaret Gray. (2003). *Honest to Genesis*. Baltimore: Publish America.

Traina, Robert A. (1952). *Methodical Bible Study*. New York: Ganis and Harris.

Werner, M R. (1929). *Bryan*. New York: Harcourt Brace and Company.

Wright, N T. (2003). *The Resurrection of the Son of God*. Minneapolis: Fortress Press.

Index